The Enduring Classroom

The Enduring Classroom

Teaching Then and Now

LARRY CUBAN

The University of Chicago Press
Chicago and London

The University of Chicago Press, Chicago 60637
The University of Chicago Press, Ltd., London
© 2023 by Larry Cuban
Published 2023
Printed in the United States of America

32 31 30 29 28 27 26 25 24 23   1 2 3 4 5

ISBN-13: 978-0-226-82969-2 (cloth)
ISBN-13: 978-0-226-82883-1 (paper)
ISBN-13: 978-0-226-82882-4 (e-book)
DOI: https://doi.org/10.7208/chicago/9780226828824.001.0001

Library of Congress Cataloging-in-Publication Data

Names: Cuban, Larry, author.
Title: The enduring classroom : teaching then and now / Larry Cuban.
Description: Chicago : The University of Chicago Press, 2023. |
    Includes bibliographical references and index.
Identifiers: LCCN 2023007796 | ISBN 9780226829692 (cloth) |
    ISBN 9780226828831 (paperback) | ISBN 9780226828824 (ebook)
Subjects: LCSH: Education—United States. | Teaching—United States. |
    Public schools—United States.
Classification: LCC LA205 .C78 2023 | DDC 370.973—dc23/eng/20230308
LC record available at https://lccn.loc.gov/2023007796

♾ This paper meets the requirements of ANSI/NISO Z39.48-1992 (Permanence of Paper).

Contents

Preface

Writing is thinking on paper. In writing books, articles, and posts for a blog over many years, my thinking about teaching has evolved into a deep respect for the nearly two-century-old institution of tax-supported public schools and its embeddedness in a democratic society.

As a teacher and administrator in public schools for over two decades and a researcher for another two decades, I have been inside classrooms until the Covid-19 pandemic shuttered nearly all schools in early 2020. Those direct experiences and my years as professor and researcher have permitted me to describe, analyze, and reflect on the complexity of schooling, especially classroom teaching. And for that I am grateful.

Usually, a preface offers an opportunity for the author to give the background of the book, why he or she has written it, and a preview of its chapters. While this preface includes some of that, I want to diverge slightly and get to the heart of this book about schooling and the practice of teaching then and now. I ask six questions about past and present classroom teaching. But why these questions?

The direct answer is that these questions capture the essence of teaching in US public schools then and now. Knowing how teachers have taught in the past, how teaching has remained both stable and changed over time, and how hard reformers have worked to improve classroom practices are starting points for grasping the largely unseen complexity, the entangled intricacies of both schooling and teaching practice.

When that complexity is fully grasped, reformers committed to improving the lot of teachers and the act of teaching can make a far better, more accurate road map to follow than ones based on faded memories of sitting in classrooms. Hence, these questions are the core of this book, each one becoming a chapter.

How have public school teachers taught?

In chapter 1, I describe teacher-centered and student-centered instruction, the two primary traditions of teaching and their many hybrids that teachers have crafted over the past century.

Have public schools and teaching practices changed over time?

Reform-driven policymakers and practitioners have succeeded in incrementally altering teaching policies and practices during the twentieth century. Chapter 2 covers some of the most significant changes, such as upgrading standards for certifying teachers' content knowledge and classroom skills; ending students' rote recitations drawn from textbooks and gaining broader student participation in lessons; diminishing corporal punishment while increasing non-physical options to manage classroom behavior; relying less on whole-group teaching by using more small groups and independent work; and adopting new technologies.

Yet amid these changes, why have schooling and classroom practices been stable over time?

In chapter 3, I look at how the impact of social, political, and economic movements in the past century (e.g., Progressivism, civil rights, business-driven reforms) and disasters such as Covid-19 have spilled over into public schools, influencing their organization and governance yet having only minimal effects upon the dominant classroom practice of teacher-centered instruction. I offer explanations for this remarkable constancy in schooling and how teachers have taught.

How *should* teachers teach?

Historically, the literature on teaching has been lopsided. The vast majority of studies have centered on how teachers *should* teach rather than how they *do* teach. Chapter 4 begins with late nineteenth-century critics of teacher-centered instruction calling for a "New Education" anchored in student-centered instruction. By the mid-twentieth century, these progressive reformers had been successful in altering kindergarten and primary grade instruction but less so in secondary schools. I then take up the decades in which civil rights reformers turned to schools to solve segregation and upend traditional ways of teaching. Following this wave of reform was a coalition of civic- and business-oriented boosters of technology in the early 1980s who worked toward having teachers use the devices made available by that technology, promising that classroom practice would be transformed into individualized learning, the ultimate goal of student-centered instruction.

In answering the question of how teachers ought to teach, the many efforts reformers have made over decades to alter traditional classroom practices underscore both the limited successes and numerous difficulties that generations of change-driven policymakers and practitioners have encountered.

How do teachers teach now?

To answer this question, I establish current patterns of teaching across K-12 classrooms in the early decades of the twenty-first century, using pre- and post-pandemic national, state, and local teacher surveys, student perceptions, teachers' reports, journalists' articles, teachers' logs, and so forth.

Why have changing and conserving been the hallmarks of US schooling and teaching?

Here I reprise educational historians' explanations for the persistent efforts reformers have made to alter schools and classroom practices to achieve their vision of how schooling should be done. Repeatedly, reformers' demands for student-centered instruction have encountered implacable imperatives (e.g., the age-graded school; traditional classroom practices; public expectations) that accounted, in part, for preserving teacher-centered instruction and its hybrids. In effect "dynamic conservatism," changing institutions and practices in order to maintain stability, has persisted in schooling over the past century.

Most readers are unfamiliar with these explanations and demands simply because they have sat in classrooms for many years taking the act of teaching for granted. Historians, however, can note what generations of students sitting at desks miss.

Moreover, this story of stability and change in classroom teaching over the past century is important not only to readers who have experienced schooling in the United States but also to those policymakers and practitioners who make consequential decisions for children. Answers to the questions I address in these chapters reveal the sheer complexity of what teachers do daily, a complexity that is often hidden from public view because teaching is so familiar to Americans. Since these questions deal with two historic traditions of teaching and their varied hybrids, I want readers to know specifically how I define each tradition of teaching.

The primary way teachers have taught and students have experienced that teaching over nearly a century and a half is what I call *teacher-centered instruction*.[1]

Features of this way of teaching are listed below.

- Teacher arranges classroom furniture into rows of desks, tablet armchairs, or tables facing a chalkboard or whiteboard with a teacher's desk nearby.
- Teacher talk exceeds student talk during the lesson.
- Instruction occurs frequently with the whole class; small group or independent work occurs less often.
- Teacher schedules activities during the lesson.
- Teacher relies heavily upon the textbook to guide curricular and instructional decision-making.

Another tradition of teaching called *student-centered instruction* has evolved over the past century and has been integrated by many teachers into teacher-centered instruction. While the teacher remains central to this way of instruction also, students have many more opportunities to participate in the lesson.[2]

Its features are as follows:

- Teacher arranges classroom furniture in ways that permit students to work together or separately, in small groups or individually; desks, tables, and tablet armchairs are realigned frequently.
- Student talk about learning tasks is at least equal to, if not greater than, teacher talk.
- A substantial portion of instruction occurs individually, in small groups (2–6 students) or in moderately sized groups (7–10 students); teaching the whole group at one time occurs as well.
- On some occasions, teachers allow students to choose content to be learned.
- Teachers permit students to determine partially or wholly the classroom schedule, rules of behavior, individual rewards and penalties, and how they are to be enforced.
- Varied instructional materials are available in the classroom (e.g., activity centers or learning stations) so that students can use them independently or in small groups.
- Use of materials is scheduled, either by the teacher or in consultation with students, during lessons.

These two traditions of teaching (and their many hybrids) sum up the ways that teachers have taught and continue to teach in US schools in the early decades of the twenty-first century.

Are these ways of teaching effective with students? The answer may depend upon how one defines effectiveness—increased student participation in the lessons? Gains in standardized test scores? I have yet to find evidence that either of these ways of teaching (including their hybrids) are linked causally to gains or losses in achievement as measured by test scores or to more or less student participation in lessons—outcomes that many teachers prize.

No surprise here, since researchers have historically had major difficulties in determining whether any single way of teaching is effective, however defined, simply due to the many intervening variables that connect a way of teaching to increased student participation in class or gains in academic achievement (e.g., teachers' beliefs, years of experience, school structures, race and ethnicity of teacher and students, students' socioeconomic status, motivation, aptitude, and interests). Considering all of these factors, anyone claiming that all teachers should teach in a particular way, or for that matter, all students should learn in a singular way is a charlatan.

As a result, avowing that one way of teaching leads to desired student outcomes remains a step too far for researchers, including myself, to take. But having detailed descriptions and analyses trumps the constant quest for causality simply because the first step in gaining a deep understanding of what three and a half million teachers in US schools do for six hours a day, five days a week, nine months a year is describing and analyzing both what and how classroom teachers teach now and how they have taught in the past.

Furthermore, in limning these ways of teaching, I want to make clear to readers that I carry no flag for either one of the classroom strategies or mixes of the two. I have documented in detail my own way of teaching history for fourteen years in two high schools and during two decades as a professor in one university. That career trajectory blended teacher-centered instruction with dollops of student-centeredness integrated into my lessons. I constructed over time a hybrid of both ways of teaching that seemed to work for me.

But did it work for students? Here again is the causality question. In truth, I have no way of knowing how effective my teaching was with the students I have taught. Yes, I have received glowing letters from former students. Yes, I have even received a few teaching awards—anecdotal data and plaques in my office. But I can also recall high school students whom I failed and who had to repeat the course with another teacher. There were students who barely eked by with a passing grade who showed up daily and did the minimum work. I have no idea how much they learned from the textbook, the course, or from me. So I cannot assess the degree of effectiveness I had with students I have taught over nearly four decades.

Yet even if I had caches of data, say, student test scores, what I taught in high school and university classrooms seldom mapped onto what appeared on standardized tests in the years I taught. And were I inclined to pump up my hybrid ways of teaching, claiming that they were effective—by any past or current metrics—that would still be a fool's errand. And at my age, I try to avoid such trips.

These points should make clear to readers that the six questions framing this book draw together personal experience, research studies, and abundant thinking about the nature of teaching in US schools over the past century. As crucial as these core questions are, however, they seldom get asked by policy-makers, practitioners, or researchers. Answers provide a first step in gaining a deeper understanding of this most familiar practice and alerting "wannabe" school reformers to the complexity of public school teaching.

Useful as these answers to my questions about teaching may be, readers need to keep in mind that much remains unknown about how and why teachers do what they do after the classroom door closes and the lesson begins. Whether it involves five-year-olds in a kindergarten or fifteen-year-olds in a geometry class, teaching is a knotty, entangled, and complicated endeavor.

I hope that readers will come to appreciate the complexity of teaching, the nobility of teaching as a career, and its vital importance to the continuation of this capitalist-driven democracy. I surely have.

Larry Cuban
August 2022

How Have US Public School Teachers Taught?

Historian Wayne Fuller describes a reading lesson that a rural Illinois county superintendent observed in a one-room schoolhouse in the 1880s.[1]

> ... [S]hortly after his entrance into one schoolroom, he heard the teacher say to the leader of the fifth-reader class: 'Mary, your class may read.' Whereupon, Mary, followed by four girls and a boy, moved to a crack in the floor that served as a recitation line. There they faced the school, and each read a stanza from the "Mariners's Dream." When the students stumbled over a word, the whole class pronounced it aloud, but when the class was finished reading, no questions were asked and no explanation given.
>
> At that point, the county superintendent took over and asked one of the girls to begin at a certain point and read to the first period. Instead, almost without stopping to catch a breath, she read to the end of the paragraph, and [a] boy's hand went up to correct her. She did not stop at "Hindoostan," he said.

Selma Wassermann remembers her first-grade classroom in the New York City Public Schools, 1939.[2]

> Miss Stellwagon, my first-grade teacher was my "first teacher."* She taught me about favorites (I was not one) and about talking in class (I was one). She taught me about keeping young children at arm's length, lest their poverty rub off on the teacher's middle-class self. She taught me that discipline meant humiliation and loss of self-esteem, which diminished you. She taught me that even if you tried to please the teacher, unexpressed standards and expectations would kill your chances of being chosen for a part in the play. She taught me that what I enjoyed most (reading) could be made excruciatingly painful, when the same story was read orally, line by line, up one row and down the other, until all meaning and pleasure were extinguished. She taught her slum children "the King's English. . . ." She taught us to sit still without moving, for

3 hours in the morning and 2 in the afternoon no matter what physical urges came upon you—for to move, or speak, or ask to go to the bathroom would incur a wrath that was terrifying. . . .

I didn't know it then but Miss Stellwagon's teaching would be pivotal in my own professional development, my loathing of her so intense that I could only become her antithesis.

I observed Gabriel Stewart, US history teacher, at Los Altos High School, in 2016.[3]

Stewart, wearing dark slacks and a maroon polo shirt over a muscled upper body, is a nineteen-year veteran teacher and baseball coach at Los Altos High School. In this hour-and-a-half lesson, he had set aside time to give a practice, seventy-five-item multiple-choice test on early nineteenth-century political and social changes and then rehearse a Document-Based Question (DBQ) in the remaining forty-five minutes. This Advanced Placement (AP) course is geared to the spring exam.

The furniture arrangement is five rows of desks facing the front whiteboard with the teacher's desk in one corner. Bulletin boards are filled with newspaper articles, maps, announcements, and photos. On one side of the room, sheets of paper carry previous AP classes' AP exam scores.

During the practice test, students filled in a Scantron sheet to record their answers to questions such as this:

John C. Calhoun's "South Carolina Exposition" was an argument for

   a. secession
   b. protective tariffs
   c. majority rule
   d. states' rights

During the test, Stewart walks around the room and occasionally tells students how much time remains to finish the test. Early finishers turned in their filled-out Scantron forms and worked on laptops at their desks. After forty-five minutes, Stewart asks for sheets from the few students who have not yet finished.

The school's student-produced video announcements come on the screen, and for next five minutes, those in the class are rapt, laughing at the student anchor's one-liners and the funny events scheduled for the next week. After the announcements, Stewart asks students to take out their devices and go to the DBQ they will work on for the rest of the period. When he starts speaking there is a rising level of talk, and a few students say "shush" and the class quiets down.

There are six documents in this DBQ. The task is to write an essay agreeing or disagreeing with the statement: "Reform movements in the United States sought to expand democratic ideals."

The documents students analyze are quotations from leading figures in various early nineteenth-century reform efforts, such as Charles Finney, Elizabeth Cady Stanton, and William Lloyd Garrison; a chart about growth of political parties in the first half of nineteenth century, and a contemporary political cartoon on the temperance movement.

As Stewart questions students, he salts his sentences with "homeboy," "dude," and "my bad." On one question about the Seneca Falls Declaration (1848), he asks what the word "domesticity" means. One student offers an answer and then, without saying that it was correct, Stewart calls on another student, who says that Mary "nailed it" and she doesn't want to add to it.

I scan the class and do not see any students off-task.

The teacher asks the class to work on filling in the DBQ practice chart with each document. "You can work together," he says. "See if you can knock out the six items in ten minutes." Students turn to partners sitting next to them or across a row and begin reading each excerpt and filling in the chart. Teacher walks around to check what pairs and trios are doing on their screens.

After about ten minutes, Stewart takes some student questions about the timed AP exam next semester. The teacher says that time is crucial, snapping fingers in time, saying: "Remember you are paying ninety-three dollars, and you spend four hours taking the test."

Now, Stewart turns to the next task of writing a "coherent essay." He asks them to begin with a thesis statement. Again, he stresses the importance of time and how each student has to figure out how long it will take to read the document, get at its essence, and begin writing a sentence that summarizes the excerpts. "You can work together," he says.

Interspersed in the exchanges between teacher and student are references to the AP exam, in particular the importance of putting in details they know outside of the document. One student mentions the Masonic political party, and Stewart says that such a detail may well convince the readers grading the exam that the student is knowledgeable about this period. Stewart then gives students a thesis statement for the essay: "Reform movements in the United States sought to expand democratic ideals."

I scan the class and see that all pairs and trios are talking to one another, clicking away on their screens, and occasionally asking the teacher a question as he walks the perimeter of the class.

A few minutes later, school-wide chimes sound, ending the class period, and Stewart reminds the class of the assignment as students pack up and leave. Three students linger to ask questions about their work. Stewart listens and comments. Students exit after five minutes.

Who's at the Center of Instruction: Teacher or Student?

At first glance, the snapshot of a reading lesson in a rural one-room school-house in the 1880s, a New York City first-grade classroom in 1939, and a California high school US history lesson in 2016 have little in common. A historian recounts what a county superintendent observed and wrote about in visiting one-room schoolhouses; the next classroom vignette is a retired professor's deep dive into her memory of a hated primary school teacher; and the last is an observer's account of a high school history lesson.

These accounts answer the question of who is at the center of instruction: it is the teacher. Moreover, the accounts share one key feature that is central to this book on the practice of teaching then and now. Separated in time, school level, and place, all of these lessons are instances of *teacher-centered instruction*.

How do you know when you observe a classroom that what you see is a form of teacher-centered instruction? One writer describes the approach as one with "[a] high degree of teacher direction and a focus of students on academic tasks. . . . Teacher presentation, demonstration, drill and practice, posing of numerous factual questions, and immediate feedback and correction are all key elements."[4] While this definition is generic, an observer who entered a classroom where this approach dominates the lesson would see and hear the following:

- Teacher talk exceeds student talk during lesson.
- Instruction occurs frequently with the whole class; small-group or independent work occurs less often.
- Use of class time is largely determined by the teacher.
- Teacher relies heavily upon the textbook to guide curricular and instructional decision-making.
- Teacher arranges classroom furniture into rows of desks, chairs, or tables facing a chalkboard or whiteboard with a teacher's desk nearby.[5]

Spanning more than a century, across elementary and secondary grades, and varied locations, teacher-centered instruction—sometimes called "direct instruction"—has dominated how teachers have taught (and, as this book claims), how they teach now.[6]

While another tradition of teaching called *student-centered instruction* has evolved over the past century and has been integrated by many teachers (but never a majority) into teacher-centered instruction, student-centered teaching remains subordinate to the prevailing tradition. Definitions of student-centered instruction vary but most agree that the following features show up in classrooms that are student-centered.[7]

- Student talk about learning tasks is at least equal to, if not greater than, teacher talk.
- Most instruction occurs individually, in small groups (2–6 students), or in moderate sized groups (7–10) rather than being directed at the entire class.
- Students help choose and organize the content to be learned.
- Teachers permit students to determine partially or wholly rules of behavior, classroom rewards and penalties, and how they are to be enforced.
- Varied instructional materials (e.g., activity centers or learning stations) are available in the classroom so that students can use them independently or in small groups.
- Use of materials is scheduled, either by the teacher or in consultation with students, for at least half of the available academic time.
- Classroom furniture is usually arranged in a way that permits students to work together or separately, in small groups or individually; no dominant pattern in arranging classroom desks, tables, and chairs exists, and furniture is realigned frequently.

Consider Jennifer Auten, who teaches second-graders at Montclaire Elementary School in the Cupertino, CA, district. She has been teaching at the school for over a decade and a half. I observed her class in 2016.

She teaches in a portable classroom. When asked if she likes working in a self-contained classroom removed from the main buildings, she says she finds it helpful and time efficient that her seven-year-olds can use the bathroom, sink, and other amenities in the portable without traipsing across fifty yards of playground to the school's bathrooms and water. Here in the portable, Auten has had her second-graders using iPads throughout the school day. In 2010, she was one of a small group of teachers who volunteered to pilot iPads in their classrooms. She has used them ever since and now has enough devices for each student to have one.[8]

I heard of Auten from a reader of my blog who introduced us to one another via email. I observed her ninety-minute class on April 19, 2016. The carpeted portable was festooned with student work, wall charts, guidelines for students to follow in different activities, mobiles hanging from the ceiling, and tables for from two to four students arranged around the room in no particular pattern.

Twenty students enter the portable at 8:30 and immediately pick up iPads from a corner of the room (there are also earphones for students to use nearby). They open the devices, go to an app where they indicate their presence for the day and choose a regular or vegetarian lunch, permitting Auten to move ahead with the lesson without having to take attendance or ask about lunch choices.

Auten calls the class to order and flashes on the whiteboard a YouTube video that shows teenagers stretching, dancing, and singing. The seven-year-olds are familiar with the routine; they cluster in the center of the room and jump up and down in time with the teenagers on the video. For the next ten minutes, there are additional videos of singing and stretching that the second-graders copy. When I asked Auten whether this was a warm-up for the lesson, she pointed out that the state requires a certain number of minutes for physical education, and while she does take students outside to exercise for thirty minutes, three times a week, she also uses videos in the morning to get her second-graders moving.

After the videos, she gathers the class on the carpet in front of her and goes over what they will do in the morning. They will write a "research paragraph" that contains three important details. Carrying her laptop in one hand, she projects slides on a whiteboard (she uses Apple TV and a ceiling-mounted projector to throw the image of her laptop screen on the whiteboard). She shows a sample paragraph on plants that the students can read—she told me that all her second-graders can read. She reads the paragraph aloud and points out that it contains description of seeds, roots, stems. She wants students to work together and write a practice paragraph on a topic they choose from an online folder called "student project choice." Each pair or trio of students will choose the topic they want to research—dinosaurs, bicycles, planes, and so on. Later in the day, she continues, each group will present that paragraph (with text and photos) to the rest of the class. She asks the class, "I am looking for a presentation that has how many details?" Most of the students hold up three fingers to show her how many details they need to include. She then turns to the rubric students will use to determine the quality of the paragraph. She flashes it on screen and goes over each part, asking students if they understand and to show whether they do or not with a thumbs up or thumbs down. Most of the students comply with hand signals. Auten goes over each part of the rubric.

Teacher then shifts to topics in the different folders on their iPads. Pairs and trios of students will choose the items to read and videos to watch in order to create their presentations. She then summarizes tasks for the class: research the topic, read materials using apps, take notes, prepare presentation, and check the rubric before they turn their paragraphs in. Auten goes over the apps students will be using to research their topic, pointing out which ones work well. After a few students identify other apps, the teacher points out which ones might cause their devices to crash. She asks if there any questions, and three students ask about different apps and what to do if the program crashes. She answers their questions and points out that if students load too many visuals using Seesaw, their screens may go blank. To an observer, it is clear that this class has done other reports before. When I asked the teacher, she said they had been assigned an animal and are still working on that report.

Auten asks students whether they want to choose a topic first or choose partners first. She lets students decide by asking them to hold up one finger for choosing topic first or two fingers for partners first. Most students want to choose partners first. They do. I scan the group and see that boys chose boys and girls chose girls. The children scatter to different tables and discuss which topics they will research to create a presentation. Students walk around holding their iPads and discuss with classmates what they have chosen and what they are taking notes on.

For the rest of the period, students work in small groups and pairs. No one works individually. Auten moves from table to table answering questions, inquiring about the topics her second-graders chose, and asking about readings students had finished in their iPad, notes they have taken. Some students come to two baskets sitting on a window ledge that hold note cards and pencils. Three boys are sitting on carpet as they read and take notes. When I scan the class I do not see one student off-task or disengaged.

Auten raises her arm and quiet descends on class as students raise their arms in reply—another signal that students have been socialized to follow. She praises students for how well they have been working on the project and reminds them that they have twenty-five minutes left to work on the projects before morning recess. Groups return to work. I walk around and ask different groups what they are working on—planes, dinosaurs (three trios), bicycles. I asked one seven-year-old in another group what a rubric was. She explained to me that the rubric tells her whether she has done all parts of the report and what she has to do on each part of the presentation to get a high grade on the report. Teacher continues to check in with different groups at tables.

Chimes toll for recess. Students line up with balls and other equipment they use during the break. Auten opens the door and leads them out. I thank Jennifer Auten for inviting me to observe and leave.

Readers need to note, however, that in both of these teaching traditions (and their hybrids), the teacher remains central to major decision-making for orchestrating lesson content and activities. What differs in these traditions is the degree to which students participate in the flow of what the teacher has orchestrated.

There is ample historical data to back up the above descriptions of these teaching traditions and their various blends. In *How Teachers Taught* (1984) and *Hugging the Middle* (2009), I collected nine thousand urban and rural classroom reports from between 1890 and 2005. I examined how teachers organized classroom space, grouped students, and structured tasks for students. I found the following classroom patterns.

Between the 1890s and early 2000s, the social organization of the classroom became informal. In the early twentieth century, dress-clad women and tie-wearing men facing rows of fifty or more students sitting at bolted-down desks controlled each child's every move. They gave permission for students to leave their seats. They required students to stand when reciting from the textbook or answering a question. Teachers often scowled, reprimanded, and paddled students for misbehaving.

Over the decades, however, classroom organization and teacher behavior slowly changed. By 2005, few classrooms had rows of immovable desks. Classrooms were now filled with tables and movable desks, particularly in the early grades, allowing students to face one another. Teachers wearing jeans and drinking coffee smiled often at their classes. Students went to a pencil sharpener or elsewhere in the room without asking for the teacher's permission.

The dread blanketing the late nineteenth-century classroom marked often by the swish of a paddle and a teacher's sneer slowly gave way, decade by decade, to classrooms where teachers were more informal in language and dress, and had a light touch in controlling unacceptable behavior.

By the early 2000s, most elementary and fewer secondary teachers had blended student-centered and teacher-centered classroom practices into hybrids.

Grouping. For most of the twentieth century, whole-group teaching prevailed. As class size gradually fell from sixty to thirty or less, the student-centered practice of dividing the group into smaller ones so that the teacher could work with a few students at a time on reading while the rest worked by themselves slowly took hold among most elementary school teachers. Among high school teachers, although variations in grouping occurred in academic subjects, small-group work occurred much less frequently.

Classroom activities. A similar pattern occurred with assigning different tasks. "Learning centers," where individual children would spend a half-hour or more reading a book, playing math games, or drawing and painting, slowly took hold in kindergarten and the primary grades, spreading gradually to the upper elementary grades. Learning centers, however, appeared less often in secondary schools.[9]

The use of student projects that tied together reading, math, science, and art—think of a fourth-grade class divided into groups or working individually on Native American life—became a standard part of elementary school

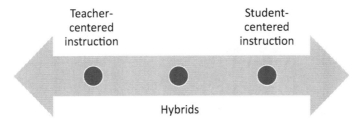

teachers' repertoire. In secondary schools, projects appeared in vocational tracks (later called Career Technical Education), such as commercial, trade, and health occupations, and periodically in science, English, and social studies classes.

Between the 1890s and early 2000s, then, teachers created hybrids. In elementary schools, particularly in primary classrooms, richer and more diverse melds of the two traditions appeared, although far fewer instances surfaced in high schools—allowing for variation among academic subjects.[10]

Even as classroom organization moved from formal to informal, and hybrids of teaching traditions multiplied, teacher-centered pedagogy still dominated classroom lessons. As Philip Jackson noted in his mid-1960s study of suburban teachers, while teacher smiles replaced "scowls and frowns" and teachers exercised "their authority more casually than their predecessors," still "the desire for informality was never sufficiently strong to interfere with institutional definitions of responsibility, authority, and tradition."[11]

And since the early 2000s, one only has to sit for fifteen minutes in the back of a kindergarten, visit a sixth-grade lesson, or sit in an AP calculus class to see, amid teacher smiles, which teaching tradition dominates the early decades of the twenty-first century.

Although much variation occurs across classrooms, teachers still change students' seats at will. They ask questions, interrupt students to make a point, tell the class to move from reading to math, and praise or admonish students. Controlling student behavior had shifted over time from finger-pointing and sneers to indirect approaches that exploit the teacher's personality and budding relationships with students but still underscore the fundamental fact of classroom life: teachers use their authority to secure obedience from students for teaching to occur.

My findings for classroom instruction between 1890 and 2005 and since then—as I claim in this book—show that the two teaching traditions at opposite ends of a pedagogical continuum seldom appeared in pure form in classrooms. In schools across the nation, where great diversity in children, academic subjects, and teachers were common—even amid "wars" fought in newspapers over phonics, math, racial content in lessons, and wearing masks during the 2020–2021 pandemic—teachers created hybrids of subject matter lessons. This was more common among elementary than secondary school teachers. In short, teachers hugged the middle between student-centered and teacher-centered practices; student participation mirrored these teaching traditions as well.

Amid a formidable array of new technological devices and software used by teachers across the nation in hundreds of thousands of classrooms—especially during and after the 2020–2022 pandemic—the two teaching traditions and their hybrids persist. If policymakers, practitioners, and anxious parents were informed of this history of teaching—and the work of other historians of education who looked at classroom lessons—would they design policies for teachers that make better use of both traditions? I would like to say "yes," but I truly do not know, because one core question about classroom teaching remains unanswered: Which teaching approach is more effective with students (i.e., results in higher achievement as measured by test scores, heightened desire to learn more, increased classroom participation, or similar outcomes).

Effectiveness in reaching desired student outcomes is what policymakers, practitioners, reformers, and parents would surely like to see, but research and evaluation studies of each approach—however defined in practice—have yet to come up with clear and reliable evidence about the relative effectiveness of teacher-centered and student-centered instruction. The propensity of most teachers to blend both traditions of teaching in their classroom lessons makes it especially difficult for researchers to find that evidence (were they so inclined).[12]

Those familiar with the history of tax-supported schooling and periodic reform movements to improve teaching and learning know that frequent efforts to get teachers to embrace an alternative way of teaching—student-centered instruction— have repeatedly fallen short. Teacher-centered instruction has been one constant classroom marker on the winding historical path of American schooling.

Most Americans, however, are unaware of the historical tensions that have risen repeatedly over dismantling teacher-centered instruction and replacing it with other ways of teaching and learning. As noted above, scholars have no reliable evidence regarding which approach or hybrid yields improved student outcomes. Nearly all Americans have had the experience of being a student over a stretch of thirteen to eighteen years, but they know little of these repeated battles fought over classroom pedagogy and their outcomes.

At the center of these pedagogical skirmishes has been the historical tension over the degree to which teachers' authority over student behavior and the curriculum has to (or should) incorporate students' interests, attitudes, and participation.

Nearly all nineteenth-century promoters of public schooling saw the teacher as a transmitter of knowledge and conveyor of dominant community values; thus, they necessarily saw students as willing, if passive, absorbers of essential content and skills that their teachers drew from the official curriculum and textbooks. Both nineteenth- and early twentieth-century elementary and secondary teachers, for example, used a standard teaching technique from the tradition of teacher-centered instruction called "recitation." With the textbook as the sole resource, teachers would ask students to stand and recite answers to their questions.

In the early 1890s, Joseph Rice observed a lesson where the teacher told students in a Boston elementary school to begin "your physiology and go straight through with it." Rice described the children in the classroom reciting in chorus, accompanied by hand and arm gestures.

> My body is built of bones, covered with flesh and skin; the blood flows through it all the time, from my heart [Rice recorded that "children swept their hands up and down their bodies to imitate the circulation of the blood and ended this part of the performance by pointing to their heart."]. The parts of my body are the head, the trunk, the limbs. . . . This is my head; I am now touching the crown of my head, the back of my head, the sides of my head, my face, my forehead, my two temples, my two eyes, my nose, my two cheeks, my mouth, my chin, my two ears, my neck, my two shoulders, my two arms, my two hands, my trunk, my back, my two sides, my chest, my two legs, my two knees, my two feet . . . and I am now sitting erect.

This recitation covered the entire body and its operations "without a single break" for ten minutes.[13]

The New Education

Beginning in the late nineteenth century, a "New Education"—as it was then called—arose to challenge the dominant way of organizing schools and teaching and learning. Countering the prevailing ideology of schools being separate from their communities and seeking alternatives to the customary teacher-centered instruction, a host of reforms (soon to be called "progressive"), spread across schools in subsequent decades to make them more child- and

FIG. 1.1. School nurse weighing and measuring pupils, Philadelphia, PA, ca. 1912. Photo in public domain. See https://www.lillianwald.com/?page_id=905.

community-friendly. Many schools, for example, became centers for medical, social, and community services, particularly in cities. Schools set aside space for doctors and nurses to examine children for diseases.

Teachers were encouraged to create lessons that crossed the divide between textbook recitation and the world outside school walls. Teachers were exhorted to get students to participate in lessons and join small-group activities built around projects that linked prescribed content to what children experienced in and out of schools. Moreover, getting students to leave school buildings to learn about art, science, history, and the community became a progressive invention called "field trips" that rapidly spread across schools that embraced progressive teaching practices.[14]

Pushing the New Education by documenting classrooms where teachers used these methods, Joseph Rice's observations of schools across the nation include a science lesson taught by Miss Arnold, a progressive educator at the Lincoln Elementary School in Minneapolis, Minnesota, where students were "almost entirely foreigners whose homes are in many instances so poor that the little ones are obliged to earn money by selling papers and blacking boots outside of school hours."[15]

The work has thus far been confined to observations of plants and animals.... These lessons occur at the first morning period, and the other work of the day is related to them. If the Indian corn is studied, the history of Hiawatha's wrestling with Mondamin may be read, Whittier's 'Corn Song' committed to memory, or the history of the plant as related to agriculture may be noted.... The animal lessons follow the plant lessons in the fall.... Living specimens are observed as far as possible. It is not uncommon to find in the schoolroom doves, gophers, squirrels, rabbits, kittens, or mice, in cages, fed and cared for by the children....

My hope in introducing the lessons was that the children from homes where poverty or heredity had made their lives barren might have a taste of the beautiful and learn to love nature.

Or consider a centerpiece of the New Education and progressive thought and action: the kindergarten. In the closing decades of the nineteenth century, groups of middle- and upper-middle-class white and black women began to advocate for such reforms in private preschools. Inspired by their example,

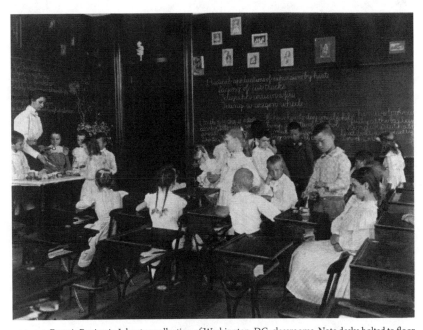

FIG. 1.2. Francis Benjamin Johnston collection of Washington, DC, classrooms. Note desks bolted to floor in rows. Five students around teacher at her desk, while other students are working in pairs and small groups or watching classmates work on project. Johnston was a celebrated photographer and journalist, one of the first women to make a living as a journalist while taking photos on commission of school districts, universities, wealthy families, and individuals. Her career spanned seven decades. See Richard Woodward, "Overlooked No More: Frances B. Johnston, Photographer Who Defied Genteel Norms," *New York Times,* December 15, 2021.Upper Elementary School Grades, White Division of schools, 1899 (public domain).

FIG. 1.3. Francis Benjamin Johnston collection of Washington, DC, classrooms. Group of black students on a nature field trip in the District of Columbia. Upper Elementary School Grades, Black Division of schools, 1899.

other reformers, facing waves of immigrants from eastern and southern Europe and migrants from the rural South, pressed public schools to implement these preschool innovations in grades 1–8 in urban schools.[16]

The multifaceted mission of the kindergarten movement sought to rescue children and their parents from poverty and crime; build solid citizens and industrious workers out of non–English speaking immigrants; uplift illiterate, rural white and black southern migrants; and relax the unbending uniformity of elementary schooling. These middle-class women wanted five-year-olds to experience life, as John Dewey argues, not to prepare for adult life. The appeal of the kindergarten, with its focus on learning through play, building blocks, songs, drama, art, and group work, attracted educators and outside reformers who saw a permanent home for this pedagogical invention within the public schools.[17]

Within decades, as immigration to the United States dipped, and generations of Americans assimilated, kindergarten enrollment reached about 40 percent of eligible children (1950). The New Education had morphed into student-centered progressivism, and it slowly became a haven for play and learning basic skills, an opportunity to live as a young child, not as a stu-

FIG. 1.4. Kindergarten class. Note that the ages of children in this class range from infants and toddlers to five- or six-year-olds. Episcopal Mission School. Proctor (Lee County), Summer, ca. 1900. Lucy Walby Scrapbook. University Archives. University of Kentucky Libraries.

FIG. 1.5. African American children, in kindergarten, learning washing and ironing, Whittier Primary School, Hampton, Virginia, USA. Frances Benjamin Johnston, 1900 (public domain).

dent focused on preparing for first grade, as has been the tendency in recent decades.[18]

A scholar with access to a kindergarten teacher's notes and records described Betty Kirby's kindergarten in 1950.

In 1950, Betty Kirby's kindergarten classroom is a busy place. The large, inter-connecting wooden blocks designed by Patty Smith Hill have a central role.

The children, with some teacher assistance, have built an ocean liner that is big enough for 10 or more children to play inside. Tickets that the children made themselves are on sale at the ticket counter. A few passengers sit in deck chairs at one end of the ship as a waiter delivers a plate of sandwiches made of construction paper. A child rolls a cart, also made of Hill blocks, that holds luggage to be carried up the gang plank to the ship. A deckhand checks the cardboard lifeboats to be sure they move up and down on the pulleys the children have learned to maneuver. Other sailors swab the decks with mops and check the anchor. The tugboat the children have built waits to help guide the big ship. The captain is at the wheel, ready to begin today's voyage. The children are literally building their curriculum as they create all they need to make the voyage a success.[19]

A few years ago, Margaret Bramer posted her kindergarten report card from 1954.[20] By then, or after nearly a half-century of efforts to install progressive kindergartens, curricula, and teaching practices, student-centered instruction had become another tradition of teaching, albeit one that was supported by many but not most American teachers. The progressive education movement in the United States, lasting until the mid-1950s, altered the popular vocabulary of reforms in schooling, curricular syllabi, and, on occasion, some classroom practices, especially in the elementary school's kindergarten and primary grades.

Yet, the central fact of classroom teaching up to the 1950s and since cannot be ignored: the tradition of teacher-centered instruction dominated US classrooms. Teacher-directed lessons with prescribed goals and objectives that involve the whole group; small-group and independent activities unfolding within a forty-five-minute or hour-long lesson, replete with nightly homework assignments and periodic tests—became familiar features in US elementary and secondary school classrooms.

A competing tradition that I call student-centered instruction, however, arose in the progressive education era and also became firmly installed among a distinct minority of administrators, university-based teacher educators, and practitioners. The slow growth of another tradition of teaching, then, makes clear that, over decades, changes were occurring in how lessons were constructed, in the frequency of student participation in classroom talk, and in how much consideration teachers gave to students' interests.

The emergence of traditions of teaching over time did not occur within a vacuum. Classrooms are part of a school; schools are part of a district; and districts, embedded in communities, follow state policies (a hierarchy similar to a set of the familiar nested Russian dolls).[21] The way these districts embedded in communities govern and organize their schools influences what happens daily in school hallways, lunchrooms, and classrooms. The next chapter elaborates on changes in the past century that occurred in the organization and governance of American schools, along with the few changes in teaching practices that accompanied those shifts.

Have Public Schools and Teaching Practices Changed over Time?

The answer to the question is both yes and no. That changes in schooling have occurred is clear from data collected over the last century on consolidation of thousands of school districts, growth in student enrollment, increased number of days states require students to attend school, shrinking class sizes, rising high school graduation rates, and similar outcomes. Moreover, standards for becoming and remaining a teacher have changed substantially over time.[1]

Also, incremental changes in teaching practices have certainly occurred over time. These changes are evident in classroom photos, journalists' accounts, research studies, and teacher surveys. Moving from total reliance on whole-group teaching to using small groups to engage in activities; adopting new technologies, such as films, radio, television, and computers; and getting students to participate in group discussions are a few of the shifts in classroom practice that occurred over decades.[2]

I take up the negative answer to the question later in the chapter, since some features of schooling and classroom teaching have remained remarkably stable over time. These enduring facets of how schools are organized and have operated for decades are essential to understanding classroom teaching.

Changes in Schooling

No change in schooling occurs separately from its social, political, and economic context. Tax-supported public schools are embedded in communities across the United States. Political, social, and cultural forces (think of the Great Depression and World War II, growing opposition to racial segregation married to political coalitions fighting to maintain segregated schools, increased questioning of authority in the 1960s) swept across the nation during these decades, influencing how Americans voted, started families, where they lived, and, yes, what they thought about public schooling. Pictures of what schools were like and how teachers taught, buried in the memories of each generation of Americans, fixed firmly in parents' minds what a "real" school or "good" teacher was well before they took their five-year-old by the hand to kindergarten for the first time.[3]

While many critics of US public schools repeat the inaccurate statement that teaching then and now is basically the same, the facts show clearly that classroom practices have changed. As chapter 1 documented, several traditions of teaching—teacher-centered, student-centered, and hybrids of both—have evolved in US schools.

Furthermore, photos of classrooms between the 1890s and 1960s show both change and stability. Because snapshots are but a moment in time, many photos of teacher and student work in classrooms over decades can only hint at both constancy and change. Photos of classrooms taken from the late nineteenth century through the 1960s surely give the impression of stability in teaching and learning. Rows of desks face blackboards and a teacher's desk. Students sit with hands clasped listening to the teacher, or they are taking

FIG. 2.1. Washington, DC, classroom, 1890s. Note the classroom clock, slate blackboards on two walls of the room, and rows of bolted-to-the-floor desks. The boys and girls seated at desks appear to have the same materials as the teacher moves along the row checking students' work. Five students are working at the blackboard. Francis Benjamin Johnston Collection (public domain).

FIG. 2.2. Students reciting at Flint River School in Georgia, 1939. Photo shows a pair of students in a segregated school giving a report. One girl with pointer tells the class about their project. Note rows of movable arm-chairs, with some students having a slate to write on (there may not be any blackboards in this rural school). Desks face the front of room. Photo: Marion Post Wolcott, Farm Security Administration, Schomburg Center for Research in Black Culture.

FIG. 2.3. Children in a Wisconsin classroom listen to lessons broadcast by radio. Photo courtesy of the University of Wisconsin–Madison Archives (ID S05822).

notes and doing assignments. Other photos show children working on activities with classmates at their desks, students at the blackboard doing math problems or diagramming sentences, and clusters of students engaged in work around the teacher's desk.

The apparent stability in classroom arrangements over a half-century, including racially segregated classrooms, however, overlooks the demographic, organizational, and administrative changes that have occurred in public schools. Educational historian Jack Schneider has described both constancy and change over the past century:

> If we could transport ourselves to a typical school of the early 20th century, the basic structural elements—desks, chalkboards, textbooks, etc.—would be recognizable. And we might see some similar kinds of power dynamics between adults and children. But almost everything else would be different. The subjects that students studied, the way the day was organized, the size of classes, the kinds of supports young people received—these essential aspects of education were all different.
>
> Teachers were largely untrained. Access to education was entirely shaped by demographic factors like race and income. It was just a completely different world. To say that schools haven't changed is just an extraordinarily uninformed position.[4]

What Schneider points out clearly are the organizational similarities in schooling and classroom dynamics that persist over time amid incremental changes that have indeed occurred in who went to school, teacher licensing, curricular content and skills, class size, and staff support for children. Although Schneider points to important demographic and organizational changes, he doesn't address shifts in administrative approaches, as seen, for instance, with charter schools.

As important as it is for Schneider and other scholars to establish beyond doubt that both continuity and change mark the history of US public schools, we are left with the unasked question: Did these demographic, organizational, and governance changes alter how teachers taught? To answer that question, I will expand on changes in schooling that Schneider laid out and then connect those demographic, organizational, and administrative changes to how teachers taught during these decades.

Changes in Teachers and Students

Consider the major shifts in nineteenth- and twentieth-century state and local standards to become a licensed teacher. Initially, local district trustees would

hire anyone who finished the eighth grade of grammar school and passed
the examination required to get a state license to teach. Then states raised
their standard to require a high school diploma. By the mid-twentieth century, teachers had to have a college degree that included education courses.
Many states required teachers to have a master's degree and pass a state test
on knowledge of their subject and methods of teaching.[5]

Teaching was a male-dominated job in the early nineteenth century, but by
the end of that century, teaching had gradually become a woman's occupation.
In the 1880s, women constituted nearly two-thirds of all elementary school
teachers and have remained dominant since then. In secondary schools, men
were in the majority until the 1970s.[6]

Throughout these decades, males exited teaching for higher-paying jobs.
Women, however—given society's view of their gendered tendency to nurture the young—flocked into one of the few occupations available to them
outside of the home. As states lengthened the school year, passed regulations
governing which schools were eligible for state aid, and standardized the supervision of teachers, the job gained respect even as it continued as a gender-
based occupation.[7]

Accompanying these demographic and societal changes were organizational shifts: for example, states began licensing teachers and establishing
uniform courses of study for students. Even as wages and salaries increased
for other jobs in the economy, however, teacher compensation still lagged behind, and men continued to exit the schoolhouse.[8]

The feminization of teaching in lockstep with the growth of state regulation of schooling were significant structural and demographic changes in
who became teachers, how they did so, and what they were expected to teach.
A female-dominated occupation tracked another demographic trend that became cemented into American schools: segregation of students by race and
ethnicity.

Where students went to school in the United States depended upon where
families lived. State attendance laws and school district policies on boundaries funneled students into different schools. While many northern and west-
ern states segregated students by race and ethnicity by custom and occasionally law, in the South, where one's race was primary, segregated schools were
the norm. Since the 1880s, for example, most cities and suburban neighbor-
hoods were racially segregated, producing schools that were nearly all white
or all black. Similarly, school districts in southwestern states such as Texas in
the late nineteenth and early twentieth centuries clustered Latino children
into segregated schools.[9]

Following the *Brown* decision (1954), civil rights activists used both direct action, such as boycotts and marches, and legal strategies to get urban and suburban districts across the nation to desegregate through busing, building schools that straddled city and county attendance boundaries, and taking school boards to federal court for maintaining segregated schools—strategies that they believed would bring minority and white children together to learn. Since the 1970s, however, there have been unintended effects, most obviously an accelerated re-segregation of poor and minority students. Few policymakers after the *Brown* decision anticipated the exodus of white families from urban districts as minority students enrolled and the subsequent return of separate schools for whites from black and Latino school children.[10]

While these larger demographic and organizational changes in schooling garnered much media attention, these shifts should not mask the incremental changes in teaching and classroom practices that escaped media attention.

Incremental Changes in Teaching and Classroom Practices

I begin with the obvious. The move from early twentieth-century formality to informality in conducting lessons became evident as decades passed.

Consider the clothes teachers and students wore in school. Just as in the larger society, customs about what to wear when and where (e.g., church, school,

FIG. 2.4. Teacher wearing jeans in front of an electronic whiteboard (public domain).

workplace) shifted over the decades. What teachers and students wore to school mirrored societal moves from formal to informal. Compare the clothes that teachers wore in the preceding photos of classrooms between the 1890s and 1940s to what teachers wear in 2022. I began teaching in the mid-1950s. I went from wearing a sport coat, dress slacks, white shirt, narrow tie, and cordovan shoes in the mid-1950s to wearing khakis, open collar shirt, and loafers in the 1970s.

Increased informality in what teachers wore during the past century also mirrored how changes in parental child-rearing practices spilled over into schools, influencing how teachers managed students' classroom behavior.

Child-Rearing Changes

Across the nation, beliefs about how middle-class parents should raise children slowly shifted from stern discipline before World War II, including spanking accompanied by emotional distance between parents and children, to more relaxed discipline in the postwar decades, including emotional closeness in child-rearing practices. One sign of that change was the appearance of a best-selling book on how to raise children.

The "baby boomer" generation grew up in homes where Benjamin Spock's *The Common Sense Book of Baby and Child Care* had parental fingerprints on nearly every page. Appearing in 1946 and now in its sixth edition, Spock's book had fewer rules for moms and dads to follow, encouraged less surveillance, more back-and-forth conversation with children, and prized closeness between the generations.[11]

Changes in parental behaviors slowly seeped into public schools insofar as middle-class moms and dads expected teachers and principals not to smack their children when they misbehaved in school. They wanted teachers to have non-physical responses to most classroom misbehavior. Those expectations influenced what happened in classrooms between students and teachers— particularly as each new generation of teachers, themselves reared in homes where spanking and slaps had declined—entered the profession.[12]

Again, classroom teachers moved from a tradition of strictly silent and obedient students with hands clasped on their desks in early twentieth-century classrooms to a new approach in the twenty-first century, in which teachers accept—even encouraged—student talk and movement in the room, small-group activities, and constant murmuring during a lesson. Were parents and grandparents of today's students to visit classrooms, they would quickly note the difference in noise levels, save for those moments when teachers clapped their hands together to gain students' attention and demand stillness.

But there were always a few students, even in the best-behaved classrooms, who challenged the norms and, in a word, misbehaved. Teachers had to deal with such students. Corporal punishment was commonly used in the first part of the 1900s. By the 1960s, however, physical punishment had diminished in many middle-class families as well as in their children's schools.

Corporal punishment, of course, is a euphemism. In Latin, corporal means "of the body," hiding that it is basically physical punishment. Rather than speak of "corporal punishment," administrators and teachers commonly called it "discipline" or "classroom management." Its purpose was to correct and deter what teachers and administrators defined as student misbehavior.

In schools, adults saw misbehavior as anything from chewing gum, one student hitting another student, disobeying teacher directives, writing on bathroom walls, or destroying school property (and many other examples too numerous to include here). All of these fall into the broad definition of "misbehavior."

Even as Benjamin Spock's influence and media attention to child-rearing practices, especially in middle-class homes, had lowered the frequency of spanking children in post–World War II decades, keep in mind that state law legalized corporal punishment. In *Ingraham v. Wright* (1977), the US Supreme Court ruled that the Eighth Amendment banning "cruel and unusual punishment" does not apply to schools hitting students for breaking rules.[13]

Schools, then, responding to societal shifts in child-rearing and growing intolerance of physical punishment of children at home embraced nonphysical options (e.g., after-school detention, suspension from school) to correct students who broke classroom and school rules (e.g., disobeying teacher directions, swearing in class, vandalizing school property).

Of course, managing groups of nine-year-old third graders and seventeen-year-old high school seniors depended greatly upon the teacher's expertise, experience, and the social class background of the students, as well as classroom size. Between the late nineteenth century and mid-twentieth century, class size ran from over forty students per teacher to between twenty and thirty in recent decades. Such figures, of course, varied by the amount of funding that states and urban/suburban/rural districts invested in local schools.[14]

Beyond class size, race and ethnicity mattered also. Teachers and principals, as historical records show, disciplined and suspended minority students far more than white students over the decades. For example, in 2003, although black youth comprised only 17 percent of the nation's public school students, they accounted for 32 percent of the students suspended. Other studies have documented the overrepresentation of black students among those disciplined. "Nationally, Black students are more than twice as likely as White students to be suspended or expelled, and in urban districts the disparity has been found to range from three to twenty-two times as likely."[15]

Over the past century, then, changes in rearing children, reduction in class size, and disproportionate discipline of minorities produced much variation in how public schools punished misbehaving students. In many districts, then and now, teachers were allowed to administer sanctions for misbehavior. In other places, teachers sent students to the principal's office. If the principal believed that paddling was appropriate for the offense, he or she would give the swats. Physical punishment was allowed through the entire age range from kindergarten to high school seniors, although the size of the latter students often reduced the frequency of such punishments. They were more subject to alternative penalties, such as suspensions from school and, for students who repeatedly misbehaved, expulsion. Nonetheless, even with the overall reduction in punishment, racial and ethnic disparities continued between white and minority students.[16]

Regularly used in classrooms and schools for decades to exact acceptable behavior before, during, and after lessons, striking students physically in 2022 occasions newspaper articles and protests.

Adoption of New Technologies

Other changes have occurred in schooling and classroom practice. Beginning in the 1980s, new instructional technologies entered schools and classrooms, eventually replacing movies, filmstrips, and overhead projectors. Teachers' and students' use of classroom devices, be they laptops, interactive whiteboards, or smart phones, would be obvious to any parent or grandparent visiting today's classroom.[17]

While the Covid-19 pandemic in 2020–2022 triggered months of at-home remote instruction and increased the number of laptops and tablets students had access to across the United States, a digital divide remained. A year before the virus hit the United States, only four out of ten students said they had devices they could individually use at their school. The digital gap between schools enrolling mostly black and Latino, low-income students and schools enrolling primarily white, middle- and upper-middle-income students had surely diminished since computers appeared decades earlier, but that gap was still large before the pandemic struck, and urban districts had to scramble to provide laptops for students without devices.[18]

One Gallup poll in 2019 of students, teachers, principals, and administrators found that 65 percent of the teachers used digital learning tools (e.g., websites, online tutorials, videos, apps, and games) every day; 22 percent said they used these tools a few days a week; and the remainder said they had students on devices at least once a week. Over half of the teachers responded that they would like to use these devices for lessons even more than they do; many students found that devices and software were fun to use, but over half of the students said they would like to use the tools less often.[19]

Like increases in the use of new classroom technologies and reductions in physical punishment, other teaching practices changed. Formal student recitations orchestrated by teachers declined in favor of oral book reports, short summaries of projects completed in school, and serial reading of paragraphs from textbooks. Many teachers encouraged whole-group and small-group discussions in settings from kindergarten "show-and-tell" circles to high school government classes (e.g., analyzing voter returns).

Why all of these shifts over time from formal to informal classroom practices, from wholly teacher-centered instruction to selective use of student-centered methods of teaching? The most obvious answer is that public schools, heavily dependent upon local financing, are (and always have been) vulnerable to political, social, cultural, technological, and demographic changes in the larger society.

Schools mirror society. Changes in cultural attitudes toward authority in the 1960s and 1970s, for example, led to increasingly informal exchanges between teachers and students as each generation of middle-class parents raised their children less strictly—remembering how their parents reared them. Eventually, many of these children of twenty-somethings became teachers themselves who approached the next generation of students with attitudes different from those of their parents.

Constant Features of US Public Schooling

Amid these varied incremental changes, readers may forget that some aspects of public schooling have persisted for decades. These stable features in the schooling of American children and youth have been taken for granted: they are so common in the landscape of public education that they just fade into the background. I have already mentioned some of these unvarying structures, such as how schools are funded and governed, the age-graded school, and unremitting racial and ethnic segregation in public schools.

Take funding, for example. Money for public schools comes from three sources: state, local district, and the federal government. Over the past century, local and state taxes on property have been the dominant way of financing US schools. Federal funds provide less than 10 percent of all school budgets.[20]

Because property taxes are the largest source of local and state funding, inherent inequities occur simply because there are high-wealth districts, such as Arlington County, VA, and Beverly Hills, CA, which generate more monies and dramatically out-spend low-wealth districts, such as the largely white county of Buchanan, VA, and the mostly black city of Compton, CA, in per-student outlay.[21]

Funding streams have remained largely constant, as have mechanisms for governing schools. While each state has primary responsibility and authority for education, every state has delegated its authority (but not responsibility) to locally organized districts (California has over one thousand school districts). These locally elected boards of education levy taxes and make policy for their schools. They hire (and fire) superintendents and their chief executive officers, and insure that these school chiefs submit annual budgets that balance revenues and expenditures. District superintendents recommend to their school boards not only all principals and teachers that they seek to hire but also what policies need to be adopted. Such governance in the third decade of the twenty-first century abides across more than thirteen thousand districts in forty-nine states (Hawaii is one entire district itself).

Also constant has been the age-graded school, a mid-nineteenth-century innovation in organizing children and teachers into units where teaching and student learning occurred more efficiently than in one-room schoolhouses with several grades. Even including charter schools, a governance innovation introduced in the 1990s, the age-graded organization continues to dominate US K-12 schools in 2022.

As with funding, governance, and organization, racial and ethnic segregation remains a constant feature of the nation's system of schooling. Although major efforts to desegregate schools since the *Brown* decision have occurred, in 2022 more than a third of American children and youth still attend schools where 75 percent of students are of a single race or ethnicity.[22]

These steadfast structures of the nation's school system affirm that, amid the many changes that have occurred in schooling and classroom practices, certain features of US schools have persisted over time.

Summary

So the answer to the question in this chapter's title is both yes and no. There have been many changes in the demography, organization, and governance of US tax-supported schools that have had lasting impacts on who goes to school, how schools are structured, and their governance for the past hundred and fifty years. Schools mirror society: they feel the effects of political, social, and economic changes that roil the nation, and they respond by adapting. A few of such adjustments are listed below:

- Court-ordered school desegregation accompanied by a civil rights movement, beginning in the 1950s but extending through the 1990s, altered substantially the mix of races and ethnicities in school districts across the nation.
- While racial and ethnic diversity in public schools has surely increased since the 1970s, the nation's schools continue to be one-third segregated in 2020.[23]
- State laws that permitted public financing of independently created charter schools increased parental choice beyond the neighborhood school, especially within urban districts. As of 2020, forty-five states and the District of Columbia had adopted charter school laws.[24]
- One constant, however, throughout these decades has been the existence of the age-graded school organization. Districts adopted this structure in the mid-nineteenth-century and that way of organizing public schools efficiently has remained intact ever since including age-graded charter schools.

Over the past century and a half, then, these demographic, organizational, and governance shifts in public schools altered substantially the K-12 system of US schooling. These changes in public schools have created over time the decentralized system of US schooling so familiar to today's children, youth, parents, and grandparents.

Far more numerous were the many incremental changes in schooling, which were often made ad hoc, piecemeal, and scattered across districts and then became institutionalized and have been documented decade after decade.

Consider just a few:

- Adding new curriculum subjects (e.g., vocational subjects such as auto mechanics and computer coding; foreign languages from Latin and Greek to Spanish, French, German, and Mandarin Chinese);
- Revising daily schedules (e.g., from 45-minute periods to 60- and 90-minute sessions in secondary schools);
- Reducing class size (e.g., from averages of 40-plus students per class to 20–30);
- Creating special teachers, programs and schedules for students with disabilities;
- Hiring support staff (e.g., counselors, librarians, social workers);
- Adopting new technologies for classroom teaching (e.g., blackboards, overhead projector; slide projector, televised lessons, computers).

There were also incremental changes that flowed directly from changes in the larger society, such as moving from formal to informal teacher dress and classroom behavior; shifting from reliance upon corporal punishment to control student behavior to more non-physical options; adding new technologies to older ones.

But few scholars have looked at whether the demographic and governance changes described above actually modified daily classroom practices. What I have found in my research is that those changes had only slight effects upon classroom lessons, while the age-graded structures—a fundamental organizational change—introduced in the mid-nineteenth century had significant impact on how teachers taught.

Classroom teaching did change over time. Teachers facing successive generations of students coming from families affected by economic, social, and political currents in the larger society learned to use combinations of teacher- and student-centered practices. They drew abundantly from what they picked up from other teachers as well as from trial and error in their own lessons. They used lessons learned in university schools of education. They scanned and adapted research findings that would fit their lessons within the constraints of the age-graded school organization.

The sum total of these changes in teaching practices over the past century and a half has been a growth of rich hybrids of old and new ways of teaching classroom lessons. The question of whether this blending of old and new, of teacher- and student-centered practices came about because of demographic and governance changes in schooling over the past century remains unanswered.

What is clear, however, to those few scholars who have observed and studied classrooms, is that significant changes occurred in student and teacher demography during the spread of tax-supported public schools into a national, enduring institution by the opening decades of the twenty-first century, and there were also incremental changes in teaching practices.

Still, overall patterns in classroom teaching were remarkably stable. That constancy in classroom lessons amid a rich mix of old and new ways of teaching is what I analyze in chapter 3.

Why Have Schooling and Classroom Practice Been Stable over Time?

Documenting that some features of both schooling and classroom practices slowly changed—as the previous chapter did—is easy to do once buried teacher surveys, practitioner journals, and actual observations of both schools and lessons are recovered and examined across decades.

Changes in every school? Every teacher? At the same time? Of course not. While the overall pattern is stability, there is evidence for intermittent, evolving shifts in schooling over the years. Establishing vocational education, for example, to connect the workplace to classrooms; creating special education for children with disabilities; adding kindergartens to the age-graded school; and starting Advanced Placement courses altered the landscape but not the geography of schooling.

Evidence of gradual changes in teaching practice is also available (e.g., from whole-group instruction alone to periodic small-group activities during lessons, rearranging classroom furniture, and the use of new technologies). All of these were documented in the previous chapter.

Few practitioners, however, have authored articles and books about what teachers do daily and how their practices show both stability and change over time. Moreover, only a few researchers have studied classroom teaching over time simply because it is labor-intensive, soaking up thousands of hours of observing lessons, interviewing teachers and, when appropriate, students.[1]

Moreover, the daily work of teachers is emotionally and physically demanding: there are few breaks and much to do at school and home after students leave school. Preparing the week's lessons, researching materials for those lessons beyond the textbook, commenting on homework, and grading quizzes and tests leave little time for much else. Time to write? Maybe during holidays and summers if the salary is sufficient to support oneself and a family. Keep in mind that writing is also no easy task, particularly if a teacher wants to reach a larger audience beyond family and friends. Writing is hard work.

Beyond structural and personal reasons, there are societal ones that help explain limited public knowledge about stability and change in teaching. For the most part, each generation of parents and voters takes teaching for granted because of the sheer steadiness of the century-old system of schooling in which they sat through classroom lessons, a system that most parents continue to support.

Then there is—let me be blunt here—the low-to-modest respect that teachers get in the United States (compared to other professions). Except for increases in public admiration during and after the 2020–2021 Covid-19 pandemic, historically teachers have scored low on societal appreciation (and in salaries) for their daily work.[2]

Part of this matter of respect is linked to the lack of pizzazz associated with the slow changes in schooling. In a society driven by constant innovation, 24/7 news channels, endless entertainment, televised sports, and the incandescent lure of financial success, schooling and teaching are yawn-producers. All of this comes to mind in explaining why so little public and scholarly attention is paid to changes that occur in schooling and teaching practices.

Sure, when district services are reduced, and school budgets are cut, policymakers and administrators pitch schools to the public as crucial to maintaining democracy. But the fact remains that schools are part of the background, not the foreground of American institutional interest except for those occasions when controversies seize schools (e.g., teaching the theory of evolution in the 1920s, religious prayer in schools in the 1950s, campus and high school protests of the 1960s, and the more recent uproar stirred up over lessons on slavery and racism and whether children and teachers should be masked during the recent pandemic).[3]

Given these multiple reasons for inattention to changes in schooling and classroom practice, in this chapter I turn to the more obvious but often unasked question: why have basic patterns of classroom teaching been durable over time?[4]

In a society that endlessly prizes change, explaining stability in any institution goes against the grain. It is far harder for historians, educational researchers, and practitioners to figure out why structures and practices are sturdy, even robustly constant over decades. And the reason is simple: schooling and teaching are complex processes deeply nested in one another and the society that provides it.[5]

Nested is a fair word to use in capturing the interrelatedness and steadiness in patterns of schooling. Each classroom is part of a school that, in turn, is part of a district, which is located in a state that has authorized local citizens to raise monies to build and operate schools within its boundaries. Classroom, school, district, and state capture the essential governance and organization of US public schooling. And that accounts only for the formal organizational and governmental structures within which classrooms exist. I have made no mention of the different kinds of schools students can attend or the varied contexts in which schools reside.

Over time, districts across the country have established different types of schools—special mission schools for the arts and for vocations, schools for children with disabilities, and charter schools. Nor have I noted the varied environments in which these schools are located, such as rural, urban, suburban, and exurban, which result in diverse racial and ethnic enrollments from different social classes. Since the great majority of students attend school where their families live, schools have remained, more often than not, racially and ethnically segregated. The nexus between state and district assessment and accountability for outcomes has also reinforced traditions of teaching.

All of these, of course, are features that touch both schooling and classroom practices in varied, often subtle, ways that observers frequently overlook. And these many factors are what make schooling and teaching not only complex but also deeply embedded in local communities. And that embeddedness within a community, state, and nation is precisely why schools bend and bow to the winds of different social, political, and economic movements as they sweep across the country. That schools mirror the nation is a fact too often forgotten by those who want public schools to be in the vanguard of reform rather than merely following it. Recall the three major reform movements that flowed across the country in the twentieth century.

In the early 1900s, progressives reformed cities and schools. When the United States got involved in world wars, schools were drafted to help on the home front as armies and navies fought enemies abroad. The civil rights movement of the 1960s and 1970s reshaped debates about social justice and launched programs to overcome the consequences of segregated schools and ill-served students. Deep concerns for the nation's economic future in the 1980s prompted school reforms in curriculum and broader choices for secondary school students.

Schools, then, are woven deeply into the national fabric. The sudden closing of all public schools in early 2020 when the Covid-19 pandemic struck the United States is clear evidence of that. Within days, schooling went from in-person to remote instruction across the nation. Thus, seeing schools as separate from the society and unaffected by political, social, and economic winds is ahistorical at the least and myopic at the worst. Schools are, indeed, nested in American society and culture.

But their deep embeddedness does not fully explain the notable constancy in K-12 age-graded school structures and the repeated patterns of classroom teaching through those grades. To get at that remarkable stability, I need to address the abiding familiarity of Americans with their public schools and the strength of popular social beliefs in what schooling is for and what it can do for individuals, the community, and the nation.

Popular Support for Tax-Supported Public Schools

Beginning in the mid-nineteenth century, Americans, initially in New England states and then the rest of the nation, taxed themselves to establish and maintain public schools. Political support for primary and, in the twentieth century, secondary public schools was evident as American property owners, both white and black, opened their wallets to pay the costs of building schools, hiring teachers, furnishing classrooms, and buying books and materials. Local and state monies underwrote urban and rural segregated schools until the *Brown* decision. In the ensuing decades, as Southern migrants came north and Latin American and Asian immigrants entered the country, the commitment to public schooling seldom flagged.[6]

Tax-supported schools, however, not only mirrored national reform movements but also echoed national and community controversies that periodically raised the specter of masses of parents taking their children out of the public schools. Such exoduses, however, seldom occurred. Already mentioned were the ongoing conflicts over religious prayer in public schools and the teaching of evolution. In the twenty-first century, teaching about slavery, structural racism, and similar topics roiled the pre- and post-Covid-19 pandemic years.

Scattered reports of parents offended by school curricula (e.g., the 1619 Project) or practices (e.g., establishing separate bathrooms for transgender students) withdrawing their children and sending them to private schools or home-schooling them circulated in the media but rarely affected overall enrollments in public schools. During the pandemic, however, when schools were closed and had to rely on remote instruction, overall enrollment, especially among pre-K and kindergarten children, did fall by 3 percent.[7]

Except for the recent blip in enrollment, US school enrollments—over 50 million students now attend public schools—and political support of public schools, even amid scattered and episodic protests about curricula and school practices, testify to the faith that Americans have in their public schools.[8] Popular support of public schools and their rootedness within American communities suggest strongly that stability in schooling and teaching practices are more than tolerated—they are the norm. Parents and voters expect their schools to have an age-graded organization, to have students who obey their teachers, and to have classrooms just like the ones in which those parents and voters sat at classroom desks a generation or two earlier. Equally important to these parents and voters is their belief in the grades of K-12 education as rungs on the ladder to higher education and financial security in the twenty-first century.

Even with an annual churn of students and teachers entering and exiting public schools, popular support of and confidence in these schools remain anchored in sustaining the age-graded organization and the familiar patterns of classroom instruction, which helps to explain the stability of classroom practices.

Consider, for example, those teachers who leave the profession or move from one school to another (about one in six teachers exit annually; percentages are far higher in predominately minority schools). Exiting teachers and the teaching methods they learned are being replaced by university-trained novices who were encouraged to teach differently.[9]

The supply of recently minted, university-trained teachers who fill annual vacancies in public schools paradoxically puts into these classrooms novices anxious to fit into their new schools who often adopt prevailing patterns of teacher-centered instruction; perversely, these novices end up becoming agents of stability in classroom practices. This brings me to the link between university training of teachers prior to their employment in public schools and what occurs when they enter classrooms as full-time teachers.[10]

University Training and Entry into Classroom Teaching

There is a historic and fundamental question facing all teacher preparation programs: do we prepare students to become teachers in schools as they are, or do we prepare students to teach in schools as they should be? Most programs have straddled the answer to the question by stressing how teaching should be and spending little time on how actual classroom teaching is (see chapter 4).

Most teacher education graduates come from university and college programs geared to producing teachers. For 2015–2016, there were just over 2,100 teacher education colleges and universities that offered over 26,000 programs across the nation. They enrolled nearly 500,000 teaching candidates with nearly 160,000 completing these programs.[11]

Research-driven universities (e.g., Harvard, Stanford, Berkeley) also have small graduate teacher education programs. But within these prestigious institutions, preparing graduate students to become teachers does not rank as high in social esteem as preparing doctors and lawyers. Scorched by decades of pungent criticism of poorly performing teacher preparation programs where professors produce seldom-read research studies, many university education departments have been viewed as second-rate within these research-oriented institutions.[12]

Universities tolerated the inclusion of teacher education because the historical function of teacher training was once located in what were called "normal" schools in the nineteenth century. These were absorbed by the next century's growing colleges and universities that aspired to national recognition.[13]

Poor reputation or not, undergraduate and graduate teacher education programs have disseminated new knowledge of the science and art of teaching to those preparing to become classroom teachers. Within these programs, neophytes were (and are) exposed to the "learning sciences"—a collection of disciplines including cognitive psychology, anthropology, sociology, computer science, the neurosciences, and instructional design. All of these programs have a clinical portion required to gain a state license that places novices into classrooms, where cooperating or mentor teachers guide them as they plan and teach actual lessons to students.[14]

In short, as enrollments in public schools expanded, and dropout rates fell in post–World War II decades, there was unceasing demand from school districts for certified teachers. Universities became the place where novices were educated in the humanities and trained in the sciences. They also took state-required courses in order to be not only eligible to teach in school districts, but able to teach effectively—as conceived by university educators—in their own classrooms. Public and private university departments and schools of education became the state-certified toll road that led directly to classrooms. As crudely put by critics of schools of education, preparing teachers was a "cash cow" and therefore essential to the financial health of colleges and universities.[15]

Many of these university schools and departments of education were places where the tradition of child-centered instruction became the prescriptive norm for beginning teachers. Enamored with the ideas of twentieth-century progressives such as John Dewey, who was initially at the University of Chicago and later joined like-minded professors William Kilpatrick and Harold Rugg at Columbia University, teacher educators began to press neophytes to embrace student-centered instruction. Teacher-student interaction and student engagement were considered markers of "effective" teaching. I elaborate this point in chapter 4.[16]

Once in public school classrooms, however, these novices, well-versed as they may have been in university programs and having spent a few months or an academic semester in actual classrooms under the tutelage of experienced, "cooperating" teachers, now faced the realities of spending six or more hours daily with one group of 25–30 students in an elementary school or facing 125–150 students in five separate classes in a secondary school and preparing lessons for two or more subjects.

Those realities banged up newbies. In order to survive their first year, they had to learn quickly and deeply the tradition of teacher-centered instruction that dominated nearly all public schools. New teachers, then, in order to survive their initial years in classrooms, had to learn different ways of teaching while unlearning many (but not all) of the methods they had brought from their university preparation courses.[17]

The literature about how new teachers survive (or not) their first year of teaching is legion. From hundreds of descriptions, one paragraph from a novice nicely captures those 180 school days where a twenty-something teacher not only encounters her first batch of students but survives to continue into a second year: *Overwhelming* is the word that best describes my first year of teaching. I wasn't prepared for the multitude of things on my plate. I didn't have a handle on classroom management, and I left each day feeling exhausted and defeated."[18] Reading that paragraph, along with books written by first-year teachers, and exchanging war stories with friends and family, one might think that most newbies quit after that initial year. Not so. Most continued to teach.

Universities and districts have tried to ease the entry of rookies through fellowship and residency programs, especially aimed at minority teachers. Such efforts, small as they are, have begun slowly to reduce exiting teachers. A recent study of 1,900 first-year teachers covering the years 2007–2012 found that 10 percent of novices left after the first year; 12 percent after year three, 15 percent in year four, and 17 percent in the fifth year—or over half within five years.[19] As in most professions, attrition occurs in the early years, but by the fifth year of teaching, the number leaving the classroom permanently is sharply reduced. By then, most teachers have gained sufficient experience in managing groups of students and skill in teaching lessons to feel competent in their profession.

In the process of surviving and gaining confidence, however, these rookies also absorbed the existing cultures of their suburban, rural, and urban schools. New teachers struggle with managing groups of children and teenagers, deciding what content and skills to focus on, and figuring out what kind of relationships they want with their students. In wrestling with these issues, newbies tossed out some of the research knowledge and techniques learned in university apprenticeships, especially the importance of practicing a student-centered pedagogy. Novices cooked up different ways of teaching learned from trial and error in actual lessons and techniques picked up from colleagues whom they saw as effective. In effect, they adopted some version of teacher-centered instruction. By year five, they have created mixes of teacher-centered and student-centered instruction that were considered appropriate by colleagues and principals. Newcomers who had been slowly inducted into the culture and ways of teaching in a school became, in time, part of the cadre of experienced teachers who welcomed and shaped the practice of new recruits to their profession.[20]

What's missing from this brief description of the all-important journey from university training programs to being classroom rookies and then experienced teachers is the decisive role that the unnoticed, taken-for-granted school structures and norms play in converting novices into veterans, thereby sustaining both stability and change in classroom practices. And this is where the age-graded school structure and its "grammar of schooling" enter the analysis.

The Age-Graded School and Its Grammar of Schooling

I begin with the structure of the age-graded school. Like all workplace organizations, it has plans for both adults and children whether they are aware or not. In short, any organization, be it the family, school, workplace, hospital, or church, has basic rules that shape what members of that organization do. The grammar of schooling refers to institutional rules and practices embedded in the structure of the age-graded school that over the past century have shaped how generations of teachers teach and students learn.[21]

Mid-nineteenth-century reformers, worried about growing enrollments in tax-supported public schools, particularly in cities, imported from Prussia an innovation called the age-graded school to replace what was then the dominant public school organization: the one-room schoolhouse. Horace Mann, Henry Barnard, and others were evangelists for age-graded Common Schools. These antebellum reformers built political coalitions in various states that persuaded legislatures and town officials to fund these eight-grade grammar schools where children ages six to fourteen were assigned by age into separate classrooms with a teacher in charge.[22]

Since the late nineteenth century, age-graded schools have expanded. By the 1920s, kindergartens, junior and senior high schools, and frequent testing (what a later generation of reformers called "assessment") became part of the age-graded system. And slowly since the 1960s, public pre-kindergarten for three- and four-year-olds has been added, as have tax-supported community colleges (once called "junior colleges") for students graduating from high school.[23] Today, most taxpayers, voters, and readers of this book have gone to kindergarten at age five, studied Egyptian mummies in the sixth grade, taken algebra in middle school grades, US history in high school, and then left twelfth grade with a diploma.

If any school reform—in the sense of making fundamental changes in organization, curriculum, and instruction—could be considered a "success," it is the age-graded school. In providing access to all children and youth, longevity as a reform, and global pervasiveness, the age-graded school is stellar.[24] Think about its longevity. The first age-graded structure of eight classrooms appeared in Quincy, MA, in the late 1840s. Within a half-century, it had replaced one-room schoolhouses. In 2022, the age-graded school remains the dominant way of organizing a public and private school. Or consider access. Between 1850–1913, over 30 million Europeans crossed the Atlantic and settled in the United States The age-graded school enrolled millions of these students during the past century and a half, turning immigrants into Americans, sorting out achievers from non-achievers, and graduating now nearly 90 percent of those entering high school.[25] Or consider ubiquity. While the ages at which children and youth enroll in schools vary from continent to continent, the age-graded school—often divided into primary and secondary years—exists in Europe, Asia, Africa, Latin America, and North America, covering rural, urban, and metropolitan districts.[26]

Why have most US school reformers, donors, and educational entrepreneurs been reluctant to examine an organization that influences the daily behavior of nearly 4 million adults and well over 50 million children, or one-sixth of all Americans in the early twenty-first century? Surely, habit and tradition play a part in the longevity of the age-graded school. Few people think about the air they breathe or the water they drink—both are taken for granted as part of living. Ditto for the age-graded school. Moreover, there are few alternatives that have lasted long enough to compete seriously with the prevailing model.

Sure, occasional reformers created non-graded public schools and similar singletons, but they were outliers that disappeared after a few years. Some private schools funded by parents and donors have remained progressive outposts, such as the Francis W. Parker School in Chicago, the City and Country School in New York City, and The School in Rose Valley (PA).[27]

What is too often ignored in explaining the durability of the age-graded organization, however, are the widely shared social beliefs among parents, educators, and taxpayers about what a "real school" is. After all, nearly all US adults—save for the tiny number who are home schooled—have attended both public and private age-graded schools. The structure is as American as apple pie and Thanksgiving. For example, when charter school applicants propose brand-new innovative schools, chances of receiving official approval and parental acceptance increase if the new school is a familiar age-graded one, not one where most teachers team teach, and children of different ages (ages 5–8, 9–11) learn together.

Not only do most Americans see the age-graded school as a "real school," but also the structure juggles the competing public and private goals that have animated tax-supported public schools since the mid-nineteenth century: preparing students to become literate, patriotic, and engaged citizens who secure jobs upon graduation or continue their education and enter careers while simultaneously promising families—the private goal—that public schooling in "real schools" will enable their sons and daughters to "succeed" financially in a market-driven democracy.[28]

Juggling these public and private aims constricts reformers' ability to try other organizational forms. State mandated, grade-by-grade curriculum standards, frequent testing, and college entrance requirements that specify which academic subjects must be taken and passed in senior high further narrow the range of options that reformers can try. And keep in mind the federal Every Student Succeeds Act (replacing the No Child Left Behind law, 2001–2015) that stipulates what elementary and secondary school grades will be tested. All these factors fortify the taken-for-granted status of the age-graded school.

The unintended (and ironic) consequence of frequent and earnest calls for radical change in instruction involving nontraditional certification of teachers and administrators, more charter schools, innovative reading and math programs, "authentic assessment," and "personalized" learning through digital software is that they all assume that such changes will occur within the traditional school organization. When versions of these reforms appear in classrooms, they often end up preserving the age-graded structure and freezing classroom patterns—that is, the "grammar of instruction." Calls for ending "schools-as-factories" are common in the twenty-first century but have led to, at best, incremental changes that have strengthened, not weakened, the traditional age-graded school.

In the 1920s and 1930s, progressive educators and civic and business leaders, for example, led political coalitions that extended public education from the elementary school into junior high schools of grades 7–9 and comprehensive, four-year high schools offering a range of curricula and extra-curricular activities that appealed to families wanting their sons and daughters to get a high school diploma, a ticket to a well-paying job. Cementing that high school structure in grades 9–12 has been the Carnegie unit, another early twentieth-century progressive innovation. The Carnegie unit required student contact of 120 classroom hours during a school year of at least twenty-four weeks. This organizational rule embedded in the grammar of schooling has become the sacrosanct standard for graduating from high school.[29]

These layers of tradition—nearly two centuries of age-graded schools—buttressed by powerful social beliefs among policymakers and parents about what "real schools" should be and by public and private goals for tax-supported schools, have combined to make the "grammar of schools" seemingly invulnerable to alternative ways of organizing schools. This remains true even though new schools, governed by separate rules such as charters, have touted their innovativeness since the mid-1990s. Charter schools have spread in cities (e.g., New Orleans, 93 percent of schools; Detroit, 55 percent; Washington, DC, 46 percent), where founders are free to organize the school, governance, curriculum, and instruction in any way they wish. Yet nearly all charter schools were age-graded.[30]

There are exceptions. A few private and public, non-graded, noncharter elementary schools—and very few secondary schools—that focus on intellectual, social/emotional learning, and real-world interactions are scattered across the United States. They challenge the existing "grammar of schooling," but they are rare.[31]

Amid much experimentation in age-graded public schools over the past century with charter schools, mastery learning, open schools, competency-based instruction, multi-age groupings, "authentic assessment," and "personalized learning," age-graded schools with their historic "grammar of schooling" still rule. Hybrids of teacher-centered and student-centered traditions continue to dominate US classrooms. Consider, for example, how the saga of defining and creating "authentic assessments" since the late 1980s has ended up reinforcing the age-graded school structure and prevailing instructional methods in US schools.[32]

Exactly what is "authentic assessment?" Following the 1983 report *A Nation at Risk*, state policymakers rushed to raise curriculum standards and increase school and district accountability. One outcome of these cascading national reforms was a sharp increase in required standardized tests. By the late 1980s and early 1990s, progressives such as Deborah Meier and Ted Sizer sought to make assignments more intellectually demanding. Students were asked to perform tasks, activities, and assessments that were anchored in the real-world tasks rather than selecting answers to multiple-choice questions on a standardized test. Meier, Sizer, and others, for example, created and organized schools where teachers pushed students to think about the content and skills they were learning in ways that went well beyond what multiple-choice items on a standardized test would capture. They also asked students to demonstrate through portfolios and performance tasks what they had learned and to apply that learning to the world in which they lived. "Authentic assessments" became an often-mentioned phrase in instructional reform.[33]

In the wake of increased standardized testing and a narrowing of the curriculum to the tested subjects—reading and math—teaching, especially in poor and minority schools, was focused on covering what would be on the tests. Standardized tests are severely limited in what they measure of student learning, much less performance. Yet policymakers and parents looked to these tests as accurate measures of student outcomes. Seeing such a backwash of problems from mandated testing, reformers saw "authentic assessment" as a way to return teaching to its progressive roots, aiming to engage students through connecting content and skills to real-world tasks, thereby increasing student participation in learning.

Examples of "authentic assessments" used to evaluate how much students have gained in knowledge and skills range from classroom experiments in science to debates in social studies courses, analysis of opinion poll data in math classes, and pairs of students conversing in the foreign language they are learning. Some districts have formalized "authentic assessments" into a graduation requirement: in the Oakland Unified School District (California), for example, all high school seniors must complete a Capstone Project.[34]

Yet as such assessments became more common in classroom and district use, they continued to be applied within the structural frame of the age-graded school. Standardized tests were given at certain grades in elementary and secondary schools, depending upon the state. Some high-stakes authentic assessments had to be completed before students graduated. Thus, state, district, and school assessments became a permanent part of the infrastructure of age-graded schooling. Such assessments continued, even when schools were shuttered for months during the recent pandemic.

In March 2020, schools across more than thirteen thousand districts had to adjust quickly when the coronavirus struck America and normality fled the scene. What happened to efforts to improve schooling and teaching practices when schools closed and then reopened?[35]

Reforms in Schooling and Teaching Practice
during the Covid Pandemic of 2020–2022

Beginning in March 2020, when the coronavirus pandemic struck the United States, businesses and schools shuttered their doors. Public schools switched

immediately to remote instruction and slowly eased into combinations of remote and face-to-face contact—students wearing masks and keeping physically distant in confined spaces—before returning fully to in-school lessons.
With more than thirteen thousand school districts in the country, there was
much variation as to when remote instruction halted and in-person schooling resumed, how many districts retained distance instruction as an option
for parents, and how many teachers had to juggle both remote and face-to-
face instruction. As I write in March 2022, face-to-face schooling has returned
to US schools.

Three school years in the United States have been seriously impacted.
While effective vaccines have become available to both adult Americans and
children above age 5, mutations of the coronavirus (e.g., Delta, Omicron)
have pressed public authorities to continue home-based remote instruction
in many districts and mask-wearing for in-person schooling. By March 2022,
nearly all states had dropped mask-wearing mandates for schools.[36] Student
enrollment in US schools dropped for the first time in years, and daily attendance in elementary and secondary schools compared to pre-pandemic
percentages has fallen from an average of 95 percent to 92 percent.[37]

In such a pandemic-shaped time, few mentioned school reform. Although
some pundits and policymakers saw the pandemic as a crisis that could leverage
significant reforms, what most Americans families and educators wanted was a
swift return to "normalcy" or "real schools." That was the definition of "success"—
not high test scores, rates of graduation, or admissions to college. "Success" was
just opening schoolhouse doors and having teachers teaching lessons.

Yet what about the sudden and massive turn to remote instruction for
K-12 children and youth throughout spring and fall 2020? Isn't that a reform?
No, it is not. Reforms are intentionally designed changes aimed at improving
what happens in schools and student outcomes. The immediate embrace of
remote instruction was necessity-driven, and replaced regular schooling—it
was a change but not a reform.

The shutdown of schools threw educators for a loop in shifting from in-
person to remote instruction. No one I know—even the most ardent cheer-
leader for online instruction—wanted nearly all US students to work at home
staring at screens. That sudden turning-on-a-dime that policymakers, administrators and practitioners did was extraordinary. Nearly all US students
in 2020 were sitting in kitchens, living rooms, or bedrooms listening to their
on-screen teachers and tapping away at their keyboards to take notes, complete assignments, and meet with small groups on-screen.

Not in any planned, intentional way—the usual way in which school reform
takes place—district policymakers across the country mandated switching to

remote instruction. School boards and superintendents became utterly dependent upon data from health officials, who themselves were uncertain about the
nature of the catastrophic plague, much less its duration. By March 2022, the
virus had infected nearly 79 million Americans and killed nearly a million. Yet,
Covid-19 was not the first natural disaster to close US public schools.[38]

Prior Massive Closing of Schools

Influenza pandemic in the United States, 1918–1919.   This pandemic killed
millions across the globe and around 675,000 Americans (ten times more
than died in World War I). That pandemic closed US schools and businesses.
Crowds were banned. Schools eventually reopened after the pandemic (Philadelphia had closed its schools on October 3, 1918, and welcomed students
back on October 28; Seattle closed its schools on October 6, 1918, and allowed
students to return on November 12).[39] And what happened when schools
reopened?

In examining those districts following the influenza pandemic, knowing
what the reform-driven progressive movement had achieved in these years
is helpful. Reforms included creating new curricula focused on learning via
projects, using new technologies of film and radio, and making schools into
medical, social service, and community centers. After the influenza pandemic
ended, schools returned to the familiar age-graded school organization and
those progressive reforms.[40]

Polio epidemics.   In 1916, 1937, and 1944, polio epidemics struck down
children across the nation. Poliomyelitis or "infantile paralysis," as it was
called, had broken out in other years, but in the three years cited here, newspaper accounts and reports document the onset and spread of the disease.
Usually occurring during summers, these epidemics lasted into the fall, re-
sulting in school closures.

For example, in 1937, Chicago, a district serving over 325,000 students,
delayed opening their schools for three weeks due to the spreading virus.
Recall that the earlier decades of progressive innovations had been incorporated into schooling, particularly affection for modern technology (e.g., films,
radio). Elementary and secondary school teachers developed, for example,
brief, fifteen-minute radio lessons that were beamed into students' homes. Six
Chicago radio stations and public libraries, cooperated to publish schedules
for lessons, with assignments, questions, and directions in daily newspapers.
Social studies and science were scheduled for Monday, Wednesday, and Fri-
day, and math and English were slotted for Tuesday, Thursday, and Saturday.
Students could use the newspaper to find the time and radio frequency to

dial up for a particular lesson. To help parents negotiate radio lessons, over twenty teachers staffed a special telephone number—a "hot line"—to answer questions.

Of course, there were complaints from parents and teachers. The lessons moved too quickly; there was poor signal reception; and a sizable fraction of families lacked radios. After polio cases subsided later in the fall, school reopened, and radio lessons disappeared.[41]

Katrina hurricane. In 2005, Hurricane Katrina flattened the city of New Orleans. Nearly all public schools (110 out of 126) were destroyed or extensively damaged. Many students went to school elsewhere in Louisiana, Texas, and other states. Some did not attend any school for months. In place of parish public schools, a system of privately managed public charter schools appeared under the jurisdiction of a state-authorized Recovery School District. Political muscle from state officials and private donors supported the venture. Except for three noncharter schools, 95 percent are now charter schools operating under the Orleans Parish School Board.[42]

What occurred in post-Katrina New Orleans was a revolution in public school governance. Instead of local citizens elected to district boards (parishes in Louisiana) to direct schools, the state created independent charter schools and companies that managed chains of schools. As for technology use in classrooms, it played an inconsequential role in these changes then and since. In effect, then, the historic shift in funding and governance that occurred after Katrina did not disturb the fundamental age-graded structure of New Orleans schools. District governance changed, but school structures endured.[43]

These prior disruptions of schools, except for New Orleans where destruction and closure of schools resulted in major governance changes, produced no substantial shifts in school organization, curriculum, or instruction a century ago, before and during World War II, or in the early 2000s. Districts mobilized technologies of the day for emergencies and downsized classroom usage of technology when crises had passed. Of note, then, is that the age-graded school withstood floods and epidemics. The familiar structure adapted, essentially remaining the primary way of organizing schools and delivering teacher-centered instruction.

Covid-19's rapid spread across the nation led to the rapid shift from face-to-face classroom interaction to remote instruction. Unlike most reforms that are gradually introduced in a few classrooms or begun as pilot projects to determine what bugs have to be removed, online instruction smacked everyone between the eyes immediately. Is this embrace of online instruction a school reform? No, it is not. Necessity, not ideology, planning, or systematic trials, drove the dramatic change. In fact, the coronavirus halted ongoing efforts to improve schooling, putting current ones in a deep freeze.

In 2022, then, with the return to in-person schooling, what reforms are being boosted? Covid-19, reformers claim, offers the opportunity to think anew and differently about the direction of schooling in America. Chances are it won't happen.[44]

Consider state tests mandated by the No Child Left Behind law (2001–2015) and the Every Student Succeeds Act (2016–) In 2020 after the pandemic shuttered schools, US Secretary of Education Betsy DeVos said states could waive tests that occurred at the beginning of the Covid-19 pandemic. With Joseph Biden entering the White House in 2021, standardized testing resumed.[45]

Critics pointed out that since the default option for schooling during the pandemic had been remote instruction, with some districts opting for hybrids that included in-person classroom lessons, the decision to give state tests and use the results as required by the Every Student Succeeds Act didn't make sense in light of declining student attendance rates once schooling resumed. Prior to Covid-19, attendance rates usually ran above 90–95 percent during the 36-week school year but fell well below that figure during the pandemic, in some instances falling to 80 percent, especially in those districts with high numbers of low-income minorities.[46]

Questions about using standardized tests were raised not only by falling attendance rates but by frequent technical lapses in remote instruction occurred (e.g., limited broadband access in some areas, defective hardware and software, chronic absenteeism during Zoom lessons, or students turning off their cameras). Such glitches weakened confidence in standardized test scores, thereby undercutting claims that tests are needed for better placement of students or district accountability.[47]

Furthermore, ignoring that race, ethnicity, and socioeconomic status are exquisitely correlated with a school's test performance, what's the point of giving the test? Accountability, the US Secretary of Education might answer. But when you know already that low-poverty schools will rack up high scores on these state tests, while high-poverty schools will perform poorly on these tests—where is the accountability?[48]

Finally, if teachers used these test scores to tailor lessons and individualize instruction for their students, that would be a strong reason to administer the tests. But they hardly matter to teachers. By the time tests are administered and results finally arrive (even broken out for individuals), those students are no longer with that teacher. They have moved on to another grade or subject.[49]

All of these shortcomings might press policymakers to drop these compulsory state tests. And were that to occur, would that constitute a reform? Yes, it would. Will it occur? Probably not.[50] Why do I say that? The entrenched mindset of both Democrat and Republican state and federal legislators, most parents, and taxpayers is that some kind of standardized test is essential to determine how well students have grasped required content and skills. It is the least common denominator of accountability. So even while standardized tests are contested, they will persist.

That mindset goes back to the mid-1980s, when state governments established curriculum standards and tests to measure students' grasp of those standards. The No Child Left Behind Act (2002–2015) and Every Student Succeeds Act (2016–) show that standardized tests remain crucial even with all of the drawbacks described above, including the shutdown and reopening of schools between 2020–2022. Yes, public support for standardized tests has slipped—especially in the final years of No Child Left Behind—still, overall, opinion polls document that the public wants some form of tests to measure students' academic achievement. And an infrastructure for testing continues to exist.[51]

As with the continuation of standardized tests across the nation, not a word have I heard or seen from ardent school reformers about altering the age-graded school structure or the "grammar of schooling." So any new and different post-pandemic ideas about the direction and quality of tax-supported schooling are dead-on-arrival.

Given the history of the basic structures of schooling and age-graded organization, overall stability in schooling and classroom practices—amid many incremental changes—becomes understandable. What is less understandable, however, in answering the question guiding this chapter about stability, has been the perpetually repeated effort of reformers to alter the dominant tradition of how teachers teach by making classroom practice more student-centered. Chapter 4 describes and analyzes the constant reform efforts by policymakers, administrators, and university academics to move teachers from teacher-centered to student-centered instruction. Reformers sought more student autonomy in classrooms. Time and again, reformers have had a picture in their heads of how teachers *should* teach. Prescriptions for better classroom teaching, that is, student-centered instruction, have been a mainstay in US schooling for nearly two centuries. How come?

4

How *Should* Teachers Teach?

The Bean

First we examined it. We found it was very hard, and smooth. When we looked on the side of the bean, we saw a little eye. The skin is wraped [*sic*] tightly around it. It is very glossy, and white. When it is put into the water to soak, it gets quite large, and it is soft then. The skin would come off easy then. I broke it open, and found a little seed leaf inside. There were two seed leaves. When we got through describing it, we each planted our beans, in a box, that had sand in it. Frieday [*sic*] we looked at our beans. We found that they had pushed the sand off of them. They were white then. The teacher covered them over again. When, we came back Monday, we found they had pushed the sand off of them again, and had grown quite large. Some of them had turned green. They left their coats down in the dirt. The stem is very large and green. The root is raged [*sic*]. It is brown.

3A Grade, School No. 10[1]

Progressivism in Classrooms

In the early 1890s, pediatrician and school reformer Joseph Rice observed a third-grade class in an Indianapolis school, where teacher and children had planted bean seeds and watched them grow into leafy plants. He saw the science lesson as an instance of the "New Education," or what historians have later called "progressive education" or "child-centered" schools, and a subsequent generation has labeled "student-centered teaching." Instead of only reading from a textbook the conditions under which beans sprout into plants, under the teacher's direction, children planted seeds, watered them, and saw leaves and stalks grow over days, all in their own classroom.[2]

That generation of reform-minded educators believed that teachers *should* guide students to acquire not only academic knowledge and skills but also connect to real-world activities by letting children get their hands dirty, experiment, inquire, and learn by doing in science as well as other school subjects.

Teachers *should* have many instruction materials for each lesson. Teachers *should* use activities for whole-group, small-group, and independent work during lessons. Teachers *should* encourage students to participate in whole-group discussions, ask questions, and work in small groups as well as independently.

Progressive educators such as John Dewey, Maria Montessori, Francis Wayland Parker, and Ella Flagg Young forged those "*shoulds*" into a way of teaching called student-centered instruction ("child-centered" was the favored phrase then) that has become an established classroom tradition of teaching in American schools.[3] Such curriculum and instruction differed greatly from the teacher-centered form of instruction that dominated most classrooms between the 1890s and 1940s.

But an example of one or a dozen lessons—see the photos of classrooms practicing the "New Education" in chapter 1—does not fully capture what the progressive movement was in public schools during the late nineteenth and early twentieth centuries.

Progressive school reforms.   In the decades between the 1890s and 1940s, "progressive education" was the reigning political ideology of schooling. Two main ideas, anchored in what had emerged as a "science of education" in these years, both spurred and divided US progressives in those years.

One wing of these progressives backed student-centered instruction and learning (adherents were sometimes called "pedagogical progressives"), and another wing advocated "scientific management" (sometimes called "administrative progressives"). They sought to prepare students to fit into work and society far more efficiently than did the traditional schooling of the day. Both wings of the progressive movement cited John Dewey and Edward Thorndike, and saw their embrace of science as the royal road to better teaching, improved student learning, and "good" schools (as each wing of the movement defined them.)[4]

Many academics, administrators, and researchers of the day glommed on to "scientific management." Proud to be called "educational engineers" during these years, these progressive reformers created lists of behaviors that principals could use to evaluate teachers, designed protocols to make both a school building and classroom lesson efficient, and measured anything that was nailed down. A "good" lesson and school were efficient, they said.

These reformers were kissing cousins of "pedagogical progressives," who wanted to uproot traditional teaching and plant child-centered teaching in schools. Their version of a "good" school was one where the "whole child" was at the center of the curriculum. Learning through experience was primary. These progressives, however, made only a small dent in US classrooms, while the efficiency-minded progressives triumphed politically in reshaping schools in the early twentieth century.

That efficiency-driven progressive crusade for meaningful, science-derived information to inform district and school policy decisions has continued until today. In the closing decades of the twentieth century, business executives, donors, and policymakers beat the drums for tougher curriculum, standardized tests, and accountability for student outcomes. These reformers wanted a "cult of efficiency"; that is, they wanted to apply scientific management to schooling by elevating large data sets and evidence-based instruction that used algorithms to grade how well schools and individual teachers were doing.[5]

Thus, the split among progressives into two wings a century ago continues to resonate with contemporary reformers. Yet the contexts for reform differ greatly, which requires a deep plunge into the history of the movement to improve public schools.

A Closer Look at Progressive Education

Historically, the many definitions of educational "progressivism" have made it a word nearly bereft of meaning. Historians such as Lawrence Cremin, Herbert Kliebard, David Tyack, David Labaree, Ellen Lagemann, and Diane Ravitch and many others have tried to come up with crisp descriptions and largely gave up. More often than not, they pointed out the movement's multiple aims and various strands—see the earlier distinction between administrative and pedagogical progressives—and then described and analyzed one or more threads woven into the disparate movement called progressivism.[6]

Progressive educators such as Colonel Francis Parker, John Dewey, William Kilpatrick, and Carleton Washburne sketched out various meanings of the concept between the 1890s and 1940s. In their work and that of contemporary reformers who embraced the central ideas of progressivism nearly a century later, such as Deborah Meier, Ted Sizer, Vito Perrone, and Alfie Kohn, we see that common tenets and practices of progressivism have turned up in schools then and now, albeit in different incarnations.[7] Look, for example, at tenets that the Progressive Education Association (PEA) published in 1919:

- Freedom for children to develop naturally
- Interest as the motive of all work
- Teacher as guide, not taskmaster
- More attention to all that affects student physical development
- School and home cooperation to meet the child's natural interests and activities

The PEA closed in 1955.[8]

But an organization's death does not mean that progressive ideas, schools, and student-centered classroom practices disappeared. Look at mentions of the phrase "progressive education," for example, in Google's Ngram viewer that includes books, articles, and other printed materials in English. The phrase appears initially in the early 1900s; its use rises sharply in the 1920s and reaches its peak in 1939. By the 1960s, the phrase again becomes popular; then its popularity decreases until the 1990s, when it again rises a tad and continues to be present until 2019.[9]

Words used in printed matter were not the only clue to the popularity of the movement's ideas among educators, policymakers, academics, and practitioners. Progressive schools appeared and disappeared over the decades. In the early decades of the twenty-first century, scattered public and private schools committed to child-centered instruction still exist: for example, among public schools, we find Prairie Creek Community School in Northfield, MN, Mission Hill K-8 School in Boston, and Camarillo Academy of Progressive Education in Camarillo, CA. There are also many private progressive schools: for example, Sidwell Friends in Washington, DC, Peninsula School in Menlo Park, CA, and The Park School in Baltimore. MD. Overall, however, such schools are a minuscule fraction of the nearly one hundred thousand schools in the nation.[10]

Beyond the small number of US schools that embraced progressive ideas, the place where they became cant was in university departments and colleges of education in the 1920s. These colleges and departments produced curriculum guides, classroom designs, and generations of new practitioners (see chapter 3). Recall that the central question facing all teacher preparation programs is whether to prepare students to teach in schools as they are or in schools as they should be. While most higher education programs include both approaches, the center of gravity in teacher education then and now continues to highlight how teaching should be (i.e., student-centered), rather than spending much time on how actual classroom teaching is done. As one professor put it, "We teach students how to become active learners, and I think that relates to the discipline problem. . . . When you have students engaged and not vessels to receive information, you tend to have fewer discipline problems." Historian and sociologist of education David Labaree calls this "the ed school's romance with progressivism."[11]

Formal networks such as the Progressive Education Association and informal gatherings of like-minded teacher educators at conferences connected college professors imbued with progressive ideas with practitioners and district curriculum supervisors. After the demise of the PEA in the mid-1950s, however, another group of ideologically progressive school leaders and university academics formed an association in 1987.

The Progressive Education Network (PEN) published its vision of the kind of schooling these educators sought:

PEN believes that the purpose of education transcends preparation for college or career. Schools nurture citizens in an increasingly diverse democracy. Within the complexities of education theory, practice, policy, and politics, we promote a vision of progressive education for the 21st century that:

- Engages students as active participants in their learning and in society
- Supports teachers' voices as experienced practitioners and growth as life-long learners
- Builds solidarity between progressive educators in the public and private sectors
- Advances critical dialogue on the roles of schools in a democratic society
- Responds to contemporary issues from a progressive educational perspective
- Welcomes families and communities as partners in children's learning
- Promotes diversity, equity, and justice in our schools and society
- Encourages progressive educators to play an active role in guiding the educational vision of our society.

While there are clear differences between the PEA and the later PEN organization in what they list as tenets, the overlap in progressive features across decades is obvious.

The network of progressive teachers, administrators, and university educators across the country includes not only associations but media as well. PEN, for example, has a journal called *The Peripatetically Published Journal of the Progressive Education Network.*[12] Then there is *Edutopia*, a magazine initially funded by the George Lucas Foundation in 1991, which publishes six issues a year and claims to reach over a quarter-million readers.

> Our vision is of a new world of learning based on the compelling truth that improving education is the key to the survival of the human race. It's a world of creativity, inspiration, and ambition informed by evidence and experience.
>
> It's a world where students become lifelong learners and develop 21st-century skills. It's a world where innovation is the rule, not the exception. It's a world where schools provide rigorous project-based learning, social and emotional learning, and access to new technology. It's a world where students and parents, teachers and administrators, policy makers and the people they serve are all empowered with a shared vision to change education for the better.
>
> We call this place Edutopia, and we provide not just the vision for this new world of learning but the information and community connections to make it a reality.[13]

In formal networks and media, reformers, including public and private school teachers, principals, and university professors, have tried to put these progressive tenets into practice. But swimming against the current of a deeply embedded grammar of schooling in age-graded schools and dominant teacher-centered instruction has been tough for these reformers.

A reasonable guess is that the founding of PEN, *Edutopia*, and similar networks of progressive educators was not coincidental but part of a response to the isolation of another generation of progressive educators amid the burgeoning, business-oriented reform movement to restructure schools in the 1980s and 1990s.

The Standards, Accountability, and Testing Reform Movement, 1980s–Present

Prompted by low scores of US students on international tests in the 1980s— *A Nation at Risk* was published in 1983—powerful coalitions of business and civic elites, fearful of losing economic traction in global commerce with too many entry-level employees mismatched to the demands of an ever-changing, knowledge-based labor market, lobbied states vigorously to require demanding curricula standards, more testing, and accountability. US presidents from Republican Ronald Reagan through Democrat Barack Obama, supported by most state legislators, endorsed these educational policies. State and federal officials aligned with top corporate leaders drafted schools into preparing the next generation of engineers, scientists, and math-informed workers.[14] Moreover, because corporate and business leaders knew that the twenty-first-century workforce would be predominately minority, they and philanthropists funded new schools targeting heavily minority districts.

Beginning in the early 1990s, under President George H. W. Bush's initiative, the White House brought together private and public funders to create the New American Schools Development Corporation. Over that decade, NASDC produced nearly a dozen "school improvement by design" models for districts to adopt and put into practice. Examples of "whole school reform models" were Success for All, Accelerated Schools Project, and America's Choice. With expanded federal funding from the Comprehensive School Reform Demonstration Act (1998) and, later, No Child Left Behind (2002), a menu of school improvement designs drew over seven thousand schools across the United States to use different "whole school models" to improve their largely minority schools.[15] Researchers who examined this designed-based school improvement model concluded, "In a few short years, roughly 10% of all public schools in the United States had adopted a CSR [Comprehensive

School Reform] design, more than twice the number of schools that were operating as charter schools during the same time period."[16] Over two decades
later, only one model from those years has survived, an elementary school
reading program, Success for All.[17]

Success for All (SFA) is largely a scripted reading program for young
children. One study said, "[T]he SFA program was built around a clear and
well-defined reading curriculum that provided teachers with a weekly lesson
sequence, and each lesson in this sequence was designed around a 'script'
intended to guide teaching activities through a 90-minute reading period. In
grades K-2, moreover, these scripts were accompanied by program-provided
curricular materials for use throughout the school."[18] In the training and
program implementation, teachers use these scripts in lessons. As anyone
familiar with putting a school-wide instructional program that relies upon
scripts into practice knows, teachers' use of direct instruction and similar
SFA methods will differ. Whether the school's teachers voluntarily adopted
the model, had substantial prior training in SFA methods, and an infrastructure of principal and on-site support shaped the degree to which teachers put
SFA into practice.

Not only did the standards, testing, and accountability movement influence what US schools did, as SFA underscores, but within the same time
frame, many state policymakers initiated a flurry of charter school laws that
allowed publicly funded new schools to be governed and operated differently
than regular public schools.[19] Depending upon the state, groups of parents
and teachers could design a new school and then apply for a district or state
charter that would enroll students, usually through a lottery. This expansion
of parental choice, which allowed parents to send their children to an independent public school that was outside of their neighborhood spread swiftly
across the nation.

By 2018, there were nearly 7,500 charter schools (there are about 100,000
regular public schools) in the United States, enrolling 3.3 million students
(over 50 million attend public schools). Most charters were in urban districts
with largely minority students. Among those urban charters were many that
styled their programs specifically to increase the academic achievement of
low-performing, minority children.[20]

Many of these "no excuse" schools, as they were labeled, opened their
doors in big cities. Different networks of these schools (e.g., the Knowledge Is
Power Program, or KIPP, Uncommon Schools, Success Academy, YES Prep,
and Achievement First) aimed at schooling low-income black and Latino
children. Longer school days, demanding curriculum, high expectations for

in-class and in-school behavior, and a high percentage of students applying to college marked these new schools.[21]

With the election of former Texas governor George W. Bush as president in 2000, both Democrats and Republicans fashioned the No Child Left Behind Act (NCLB), wrapping these state and local efforts into national policy. According to surveys of teachers and reports from researchers, policymakers, and journalists, the standards, testing, and accountability movement has strongly influenced classroom content and practices in the 1990s and especially since NCLB became law in 2001.

Teachers reported spending more classroom time preparing students for state tests and less time on those subjects not on tests (e.g., science, social studies). Journalists uncovered that middle and high school students who scored poorly on tests had to double up on reading and math periods and could no longer take other academic subjects. Prodded by district, state, and federal officials, teachers used phonics in primary grade classrooms. According to observers, lecturing and assigning more homework from textbooks had become pervasive in secondary schools. These reform-driven shifts in schooling and classroom practice over two decades reinforced the existing tradition of teacher-centered instruction.[22]

Progressives Still Active during NCLB and Standards Movement

There were progressives who pushed back against this standards movement by speaking out and creating another generation of progressive schools and classroom practices in big cities. A surge of urban small schools, including charters, arose in the late 1980s and subsequent decades.[23]

Consider Deborah Meier and her colleagues' creation of Central Park East Secondary in New York City in the mid-1980s and the subsequent flurry of high schools that reorganized into small academies within the same building. Propelled by donors and urban educators who saw large urban high schools (i.e., fifteen hundred students or more) as alienating to both students and teachers, a raft of secondary small schools arose and gained prominence as both academically high achieving and engaging for students who came to know their classmates. These smaller secondary schools, including charters, were connected in spirit and practices with alternative schools founded in the 1960s and 1970s but, more importantly, drew from earlier progressive ideas and school practices.[24]

And there were some progressive state policymakers who tried to combine both adhering to NCLB and creating non-graded schools. School reform in Kentucky since the 1990s, for example, illustrates that what happened in one state could stir ripples across the country.

Kentucky School Reform, 1990s

In 1989, the Kentucky Supreme Court ruled in *Rose v. Council for Better Education* that the state system of schooling was unconstitutional in both its funding and operating of public schools. Schools, they ordered, had to be equitably funded and operated across Kentucky's 120 counties. The next year, the General Assembly, led by the Prichard Committee, passed the comprehensive Kentucky Educational Reform Act (KERA). The law increased funding, reorganized school governance, required accountability by focusing on student performance, reduced nepotism and corruption, and added a raft of new programs.[25]

One of those changes embedded in KERA echoes the continuation of the progressive tradition. Primary grades (1–3) in elementary schools across Kentucky had to be non-graded until the fourth grade. Progressive educators in the state and elsewhere applauded the concept and program. These non-graded primary classrooms were supposed to include seven "critical attributes": "developmentally appropriate educational practices, multi-age/multi-ability classrooms, continuous progress, authentic assessment, qualitative reporting methods, professional teamwork, and positive parent involvement."[26] What and how teachers were supposed to teach six- through nine-year old children were left to administrators and practitioners to work out in each of Kentucky's elementary schools, especially the demand that teachers use "authentic assessment" (see chapter 3). Teachers knew that the state test would be given in the fourth grade. For example, in addition to the state standardized test, fourth-grade teachers were asked to "authentically assess" Kentucky students. Teachers collected portfolios eight times a year; these portfolios had to include six different pieces or types of student writing.[27]

While the state department of education issued directives and suggestions encouraging student-centered instruction in the non-graded primary schools, what occurred during classroom lessons was handcrafted by teachers and school principals. Variation in what was designed and eventually implemented, of course, was rampant.[28]

By 1998, however, the non-graded primary had become less attractive as an option for both Kentucky educators and parents. Implementation of the program had varied across the state: many schools partially implemented the innovation and customized it to fit their context, while others ignored it completely. Moreover, growing concern for higher academic achievement and test scores among legislators, educational policymakers, and school practitioners eroded interest in the non-graded primary. Teachers and principals in these elementary schools also found the work very demanding, requiring extra time before and after school to prepare instructional materials for the different activities that teachers orchestrated.[29] In other states, independent public charter schools might have provided a home for the non-graded primary, but Kentucky did not allow charter schools until 2017 and has yet to provide funding for such schools.[30]

As had occurred repeatedly when political and socioeconomic movements had swept across the United States, state and district policymakers reacted by mandating top-down policies. So, too, with the business-oriented drive to raise curriculum standards, increase test scores, and hold districts and schools accountable for what students achieved. The central belief since the late 1980s that such academic outcomes would spike higher percentages of students prepared to enter higher education and the workplace remains firm and strong as I write in 2022.

But what about persistent beliefs among progressives of what a "good" school is and what effective teaching and learning are? Did they survive? The history I have recounted thus far leads me to say yes. As in the past, progressive ideas and practices that include deeply rooted views about what are "good" schools and "good" lessons have not disappeared. Both are present in US schools today, although the organization of schooling—the age-graded school—remains intact, as does teacher-centered instruction.

What has happened over time is that incremental changes in schools, due to national social, economic, and political movements over the past century (e.g., progressive, civil rights, and business-driven reforms) have pushed educators to amend, modify, and create small but important changes in both schooling and classroom practice. By the early decades of the twenty-first century, many urban districts had created alternatives to the neighborhood school, such as magnets and charters, that gave parents wider choices of where to send their children. New Orleans, Chicago, Washington, DC, and New York City—to cite a few examples—had scores of open-enrollment schools where parents could register their sons and daughters. Schools that offered traditional, progressive, and hybrid approaches enlarged the menu of choices available to parents.

Another crucial change has been the melding of two teaching traditions as generations of teachers integrated some student-centered practices into the dominant teacher-centered tradition of teaching. Yet, as this slow integration in teaching practice occurred, current progressive school reformers had to contend with the existing system of schooling. They had to grapple with the age-graded school and its "grammar of schooling" that had been in place since the mid-nineteenth century.

Growth of Hybrid Teaching Practices

What has resulted from the past and current struggles between educational progressives committed to the tradition of student-centered instruction and conservatives bound to teacher-centered instruction is a slow growth of hybrid teaching practices. Over the past century, the emergence of such hybrids during and after surges of progressive ideas and practices has tamped down any public fuss that might have occurred over different conceptions of "good" teaching. Thus, hybrids became nests where progressive instruction occupied space within the dominant teacher-centered tradition of classroom practice.

THREE EXAMPLES

I begin with my experiences as a high school history teacher. The late 1960s and early 1970s were years of instructional innovation that got much media attention. Widespread, hyped-up talk flourished among policymakers who banged drums for teachers to adopt student-centered practices such as "individualized learning" and "differentiated instruction."

One popular technique bandied about by progressive practitioners and administrators of the day was linked to both of these phrases: "learning centers." Used by many elementary school teachers, learning centers (later called "learning stations") enabled primary-grade children to rotate through a handful of centers (e.g., blocks, books, dramatic play, art, science, math) during portions of the school day.[31]

With older students, secondary academic teachers, including myself, commonly taught up to five forty-five-minute periods a day. By the late 1960s, I had already taught high school history and social studies for a dozen years in both Cleveland and Washington, DC. After directing a school-based teacher-training project in a DC school, I returned to teaching five classes of US history at Roosevelt High School. Teaching five classes a day is a grind. Even with my years of experience and using shortcuts I had learned in preparing lessons and finding materials, teaching five lessons wore me out by day's end. I used mini-lectures, borrowed questions from US history textbooks, conducted whole-group discussions, and, on occasion, broke the class into small groups to work on assigned tasks and give group reports. By that time in my career I had already developed a hybrid of the two teaching traditions that bore my signature.

Because of my prior experiences in the District of Columbia training teams of new young teachers, Maxine Daly, a former colleague of mine at nearby Cardozo High School and director of the DC Urban Teacher Corps, asked me to train four entry-level teachers of English and social studies assigned to Roosevelt High School.

I agreed and my teaching load of five history classes was reduced to two US history courses. Now with a reduced teaching schedule and overseeing a team of novices, I wanted to experiment in my two classes with other ways of getting students to inquire, think, and work together. Very much taken by talk of "learning centers" in high school classrooms—I had observed such activities in a few DC elementary schools in the mid-1960s when I directed a school-based teacher-training program—I decided to set up "learning centers" in both of my eleventh-grade US history classes during a unit on industrializing America in post–Civil War decades.[32]

Those were the years when scrappy entrepreneurs, such as John D. Rockefeller, Andrew Carnegie, and Philip Armour, amassed enormous personal wealth by creating monopolies in such industries as oil, steel, and meatpacking. The great wealth these magnates accumulated led to Rockefeller and others establishing charitable foundations that donated money to worthwhile causes. There was a moral dilemma buried in the methods these men used to become rich and then turn around to give away much of their fortune that I wanted my students to consider and judge.

Rockefeller, for example, was a self-made entrepreneur who created Standard Oil, a company whose activities eventually included extracting crude oil from the ground, refining that oil, and distributing many products—from kerosene for lamps to asphalt and lubricants—to stores and households. By 1880, the company controlled 90 percent of the petroleum business in the nation.[33] Standard Oil set prices for oil products because Rockefeller and his family had the drive, resources, and moxie to do exactly that. Not until the early twentieth century did the federal government begin to crack down on monopolies setting prices that gouged the public.

By the 1890s, Rockefeller had already created one of America's largest fortunes. He then left operating the company to family members and established foundations to give away a large portion of that fortune.[34] I wanted students to consider the moral dilemma of industrial entrepreneurs who amassed huge wealth by crushing competitors and charging consumers high prices, and then decided to give away much of what they had accrued. Does giving to charities erase the corner-cutting tactics used to accumulate their wealth? Does doing good erase doing bad? This was the heart of the unit on John D. Rockefeller that I taught in the early 1970s.

For part of that unit, I set up multiple "learning centers" once a week for each of my two classes during a fifty-minute period. Each class had about thirty eleventh-grade students, with about twenty attending on any given day. Here's how the "learning centers" worked. Prior to setting up the learning centers, students had read the few textbook pages on Standard Oil and Rockefeller becoming a philan-thropist. They were assigned questions to answer about the many uses of crude oil once it was refined, how railroads and tankers transported oil to cities and towns, the ways that Standard Oil crushed competing small producers and refiners, and the lives of the Rockefellers before and after they became millionaires.

To set up the learning centers in the two classes, I rearranged the rows of mov-able desks to make clusters in the middle of the room, leaving sufficient space for students to move around the periphery of the room from wall to blackboard and to a wall upon which I had taped posters, blank white sheets, and tasks for stu-dents to work on when they arrived at each center. For example, one center had a projector loaded with a filmstrip on Rockefeller and the establishment of Standard Oil. Each student would pick up a ditto sheet of questions. Students were asked to determine who the authors of the filmstrip were, their credentials, how credible their descriptions of the founder and his company were, and whether they de-tected any bias in the filmstrip toward or against Rockefeller. The students worked in pairs, trios, or alone to write down their answers.

Another center had a brief article from muckraking journalist Ida Tarbell, who exposed Standard Oil and the tactics Rockefeller and company executives used to create a monopoly on the sale of oil products to Americans. Standard Oil bought up rival companies, pressured railroad owners to charge Standard Oil less to ship oil than competitors' products. Moreover, the company drove out these rivals by lowering prices and then later raising them after these companies closed. Again, the questions got at the credibility of the author, any slant toward or against Rock-efeller, and the tactics the company used.

Then there was an activity that displayed a list of Rockefeller gifts to medi-cal, educational, and religious organizations and individuals. Dollar amounts that flowed to these organizations and how much they spent were taped to the walls. The students' ditto sheet asked for two written paragraphs with examples to back up what the student judged to be important in the Rockefeller grant he or she decided to write about.

The final center contained photos of Rockefeller's family, their homes, cars, and personal lives, along with testimonials from grantees of how the monies they received changed their lives. The ditto sheet assigned the student to write a two-page essay answering the question of whether Rockefeller's good deeds and the millions of dollars he gave to others erased his brutal business tactics in creating the Standard Oil.

Once every two weeks I constructed these learning centers on different topics for the rest of the school year. Doing so took a tremendous amount of my time. I had to find materials, figure out the questions I would ask, set up the actual centers, using the limited technologies I had at the time, and read and grade the ditto sheets that students turned in as their homework.

I could create these learning centers in my teaching repertoire only if I had a reduced teaching load—in this case two classes a day. For the rest of the week, my teaching included the familiar array of lesson techniques that made my approach a hybrid of teacher-centered and student-centered traditions that evolved over a dozen years. That was what one history and social studies teacher with a reduced teaching load did between the late 1960s and early 1970s.

Every teacher then and now within the structure of the age-graded school has tailored their blending of teaching traditions into a unique repertoire. As I described above, I mixed elements of both teaching traditions into my unique blend. Now, fast-forward to two contemporary teachers and my observations of their lessons.

OTHER HYBRIDS

In 2019, I visited a chemistry class in a "pilot school" called Social Justice Humanities Academy (SJHA) located in the Los Angeles Unified School District. Here is what I saw in one classroom within a largely working-class Latino school that prepared students who would be the first in their families to attend college.

Brenda Arias teaches chemistry first period of the day—from 8:30 to 10:21 (most of the other periods in the day run about an hour and a half). This is her fifth year at SJHA.

The thirty-one students—the largest class I have observed at SJHA—mostly tenth-graders, are also having breakfast at the beginning of the first period of the day. Two students had gone to the cafeteria and brought back milk, juice, cereal, and egg sandwiches for the entire class. Students picked what they wanted, and they spread out among lab tables to eat and talk. This occurs every morning at SJHA.

After breakfast, students toss trash in a can and pick up Chromebooks from a cart to take back to their lab tables. All tables holding 2–3 students face the whiteboard and teacher desk—also a lab table. As Arias takes roll, I look around the room and see wall posters displaying a list of "Habits of Mind" and "Common Core Mathematical Practice Standards," college banners, and the obligatory Periodic Elements chart for a chemistry course. A teacher aide is in the room because there are a half-dozen students with disabilities that will need help with the lesson. He circulates and talks to particular students about the tasks they have to work on.

Arias tells class what's due today and during the week. "I need you to look at me," she says. "I need you to focus." Most of the class will be taking a twenty-minute practice test for a later exam that will improve their low scores over the first time they took the test. All of the practice questions and answers are loaded on the Chromebook. I observe the entire class beginning to work.

Some students partner up, and others work in small groups or alone at different tables. A nearby student shows me the questions and correct answers on her screen as Arias walks around the room checking students' work and answering questions. I scan the class and see everyone clicking away on their devices.

Arias then asks class to close Chromebooks and return to their seats. She tells class that they must have the practice test completed by Thursday or "you get . . ." She pauses and several students say, "a zero."

She then segues to next part of lesson. "Ladies and Gentlemen, we are going over 4.3 homework. Log on to 4.3 and we will go over 7, 10, and 11 because I made mistakes and want to correct them." The number (4.3) the teacher calls out corresponds to a text chapter on gases and solids and worksheets that are loaded on the Chromebooks and assigned as homework.

A loud hum arises in class. Arias says, "Everyone calm down. If you didn't do homework, what will you get?" Class responds: "A zero." Students also know that teacher gives them three chances to do homework correctly.

She goes over the incorrect answers on the whiteboard at front of the room and asks class to correct them. On one of the corrections about the temperature of a gas compared to a solid, she says, "My knucklehead move was the wrong answer." She says, "I'm sorry. Everyone makes mistakes."

Arias asks students to pair up and make corrections. As they do, they complete homework on the Chromebook.

The students I observed in the class pay attention to what the teacher said and respond to her requests. I saw no students with their heads on desks, students playing with devices, or whispered conversations among the tenth-graders.

Another example of hybrid teaching I observed was in a second-grade classroom in an affluent Bay Area school district.

Jennifer Auten, a thirteen-year veteran, teaches second-graders in a portable classroom at Montclaire Elementary School in the Cupertino, CA, district. She likes working in a self-contained classroom removed from the main building. She finds it time-efficient that her seven-year-olds can use the bathroom, sink, and other amenities in the portable without traipsing across fifty yards of playground to the school's bathrooms and water fountains.

I observed her ninety-minute class in April 2016. The carpeted portable was festooned with student work, wall charts, and guidelines for students to follow in different activities, and mobiles hanging from ceiling. Tables for 2–4 students were arranged around the room in no particular pattern.

Twenty students enter the portable at 8:30 and immediately pick up iPads from a corner of room (there are also earphones for students to use). They open the devices, go to an app where they indicate their presence for the day, and choose a regular or vegetarian lunch, permitting Auten to move ahead with the lesson without stopping the class to take attendance or ask about lunch choices.

Auten calls the class to order and flashes on whiteboard a YouTube video that shows teenagers stretching, dancing, and singing. The seven-year-olds are familiar with the routine; they cluster in the center of the room and jump up and down in time with the teenagers on the video.

For the next ten minutes, there are additional videos of singing and stretching that the second-graders copy. When I asked Auten whether this was a warm-up for the lesson, she pointed out that the state requires so many minutes of time in physical education, and while she does take students outside to exercise for thirty minutes three times a week, she also uses videos in the morning to get her second-graders moving.

After the videos, she gathers the class on the carpet in front of her and goes over the morning schedule. They will write a "research paragraph" that contains three important details.

Carrying her laptop in one hand, she projects slides on a whiteboard (she uses a ceiling-mounted projector to throw images from her laptop screen onto the whiteboard). She shows a sample paragraph on plants that the students can read—she told me that all her second-graders could read. She reads the paragraph aloud and points out that it contains a description of seeds, roots, and stems. She wants students to work together and write a practice paragraph on a topic they choose from an online folder called "student project choice."

Each pair or trio of students will choose the topic they want to research—dinosaurs, bicycles, planes, etc. Later in the day, she continues, each group will present that paragraph (with text and photos) to the rest of the class. She asks class, "I am looking for a presentation that has how many details?" Most of the students hold up three fingers to show her how many details they need to include.

She then turns to the rubric students will use to determine the quality of the paragraph. She flashes it on screen and goes over each part, asking whether students understand and to show whether they do or do not by thumbs up or thumbs down. Most of the students comply with hand signals. Auten goes over each part of the rubric.

Teacher then shifts to topics in the different folders on their iPads from which pairs and trios of students will choose the items to read and videos to watch in order to create their presentations.

She then summarizes tasks for the class: research the topic, read materials using apps, take notes, prepare presentation, and check the rubric before they turn it in. Auten then goes over the apps students will be using to research their topic (e.g., Epic!, Zaption), pointing out which ones work well. She then points out which apps might cause their devices to crash.

She asks if there are any questions and three students ask about different apps and what to do if the program crashes. She answers their questions and points out that if students load too many visuals using the Seesaw app, the program may crash.

Auten then asks students whether they want to choose a topic first or choose partners first. She lets students decide by asking them to hold up one finger for choosing topic first or two fingers for partners first. Most students want to choose partners first. They do. I scan the group and see that boys chose boys and girls chose girls. The children scatter to different tables and discuss which topics they will research and create a presentation. Students walk around holding their iPads and discuss with classmates what they have chosen and what they are taking notes on.

For the rest of the period, students work in small groups and pairs. No one works individually. Auten moves from table to table answering questions, inquiring about topics second-graders chose, and asking about readings students had finished in their iPad and notes they have taken. Some students come to two baskets sitting on a window ledge that hold note cards and pencils. Three boys are sitting on carpet as they read and take notes. When I scan the class, I do not see one second-grader off-task or disengaged.

Auten raises her arm and quiet descends on class as students raise their arms in reply. She praises students for how well they have been working on project and reminds them that they have twenty-five minutes left to work on the projects before morning recess. Groups return to work.

I walk around and ask different groups what they are working on—planes, dinosaurs (three trios), bicycles. I asked one seven-year-old in another group what a rubric was. She explained to me that the rubric tells her whether she has done all parts of the report and what she has to do on each part of the presentation to get a high grade. Teacher continues to check in with different groups at tables.

Chimes toll for recess. Students line up with balls and other equipment they use during recess.

These three examples of how I slowly developed a hybrid of teaching traditions in my history classes a half-century ago, a report of observing a second-grade lesson, and a high school chemistry class six years ago, in my judgment, illustrate the presence of hybrid ways of teaching after reformers then and now have tried to combine progressive ideas and practices with teacher-directed instruction. That these lessons also show the widespread integration of technologies into daily routines suggests that access to and use of personal computer devices have become an established pattern in instructing students in the past two decades.

Thus, these hybrid methods of teaching, like so many others in US schools, reveal how progressive instruction or, as Joseph Rice put it a century ago, the "New Education," has come to nest within the dominant teacher-centered tradition of classroom practice.[35] Recall the very beginning of this chapter, where Joseph Rice describes a lesson he observed in the 1890s that characterized the "New Education." A third-grade student in an Indianapolis elementary school reported how he and classmates had planted beans and what happened to the seeds as they grew. No surprise, then, that this teacher well over a century ago was already blending two traditions of teaching and that such a school activity continues into the present day.

Based upon my historical research on teaching and direct experience in schools and classrooms, previous chapters have documented blends of two traditions of teaching that have, over time, emerged in US classrooms. So what is the answer to the chapter question: How should teachers teach?

The dominant way of teaching has been teacher-centered. That way was challenged by progressive educators a century ago, and features of student-centered instruction have slowly been integrated into teachers' repertories since then. Thus, hybrids blending both teaching traditions have evolved out of actual experiences in America's age-graded elementary and secondary school classrooms. The only *should* about classroom teaching that exists is in the abiding rhetoric of those academics, policymakers, and practitioners who have held on to the dream of child-centered instruction that progressive reformers of the early twentieth century had laid out for all educators to pursue.

Distinguishing between passionate reformers' talk about how teachers *should* teach and how teachers *do* teach after they close the classroom door is what I have tried do thus far in this book. The next chapter continues that quest of capturing how teachers teach by describing and analyzing how teachers have taught in the past few years.

How Do Teachers Teach Now?

Answering the question is not easy in 2022. The Covid-19 pandemic has spiked repeatedly over the past two years as mutations of the virus have swept across the nation, infecting millions. The World Health Organization began naming variants of the coronavirus with letters from the Greek alphabet. As the mutation has spread across the globe, Americans have become familiar with Greek letters.[1]

As each variant popped up, schools affected by temporary closures relied upon students receiving homebound lessons on computers. Inequalities in funding and operating urban and rural schools located in districts where poor parents lived became all too glaringly exposed once schools closed. Many districts that had fed breakfast and lunch to low-income minority students prior to Covid-19 either stopped doing so or had families come to school to pick up food. Districts distributed devices to those students who lacked home computers.[2]

Some districts and schools did stay open during a spike in infections while taking precautions with masks, physical distancing, and improved ventilation. By January 2022, nearly 90 percent of public schools were open for face-to-face instruction. Getting a clear, precise answer to how teachers across over thirteen thousand school districts in the United States managed their lessons remains difficult, given the repeated surges of the virus and fragmentary reports.

Moreover, the lack of data on teaching practices before, during, and after the pandemic leaves any answer wobbly. Chapter 4 dealt with the massive amount of writing by both researchers and practitioners about how teachers *should* teach. But how teachers *do* teach daily lessons in recent years remains unanswered. Given these limitations, in this chapter I decided to define current teaching as what teachers did in their classrooms between 2005–2022.[3]

Even in this past decade and a half, reliable descriptions of classroom lessons and surveys of teaching practices are tough to find. Sure, there are journalists who have gone into classrooms and reported what they saw. And there are teachers who recounted their lessons in blogs, social media, and articles. And, yes, there have been scattered and episodic surveys of teachers that described classroom practices, and there have been students who report on how their teachers teach.[4]

Like most surveys, however, these are suspect because they depend upon self-reports that more often than not conflict with one another and, even worse, are unrepresentative of a state's or nation's teachers. Hence, answering the question of how teachers have taught since 2005 including the pandemic, remains a challenge.[5]

Occasional firsthand accounts from teachers do appear and help provide textual evidence for what occurs in many classrooms. For example, when the pandemic struck in early 2020, Carly Berwick, then a New Jersey high school humanities teacher and mother of elementary school students, captured well the shock of switching instantly from face-to-face classroom teaching to remote instruction.

> Teachers like me are now preparing, in earnest, to teach remotely, a new circumstance that adds more work to our normal planning load. We are tasked with developing and posting two weeks of extra online lesson plans in case we take ill ourselves, along with daily plans with activities and assessments to get us through the next few weeks. Quizzes and tests that can be gamed by googling the answers are out; reflections and open-book writing tasks are in. In a strange way, we are excited, though exhausted, to take our existing curriculum and try something new.
>
> In our district training yesterday, pulled together by hyper-organized lead teachers, we learned we should post agendas and do-nows every day, appear online with our students during a shortened regular class schedule, take roll virtually, have a daily exit ticket or other form of assessment, and figure out ways to make the online content intriguing.
>
> It's a lot to process, but my colleagues are keeping their spirits up and collaborating to share what they know. During the training, teachers turned to one another to trade tips, showing each other how to time postings and upload folders in our learning management system (LMS). I'm glad to have some guidance for this new world, even if we're all really figuring things out as we go along. . . .
>
> I wonder how we will be able to make instruction clear without being able to look kids in the face. Will we be able to detect and redirect students who are spinning their wheels? Will we even be able to tell how many kids are paying attention, or falling hopelessly behind? And if we do pull this all off,

FIG. 5.1. Child in a remote lesson (public domain).

what does that mean about the relevance of in-person teaching and the school community at-large? . . .

But nearby, at my own children's K-8 school, where half of the students receive free- and reduced-priced lunch, the upside feels more tenuous, and the questions are cause for concern. Many students don't have computers or Internet at home, a stark reality for many schools around the nation. Parents worry about how they will work if children need supervision or how hungry children will get meals. So far, their school, and the larger district are xeroxing hardcopy packets; my son's fifth-grade teacher told them to bring home their textbook every day, in the event they can't return. They still live in uncertainty, not knowing when schools will close, and facing a different, more urgent set of circumstances in the event they do.[6]

While researchers documented students' "learning loss" from school closures, what children learned from remote instruction during the pandemic is yet largely unknown.[7] Across the country from Carly' Berwick's high school, an Oregon teacher describes her experience teaching both online and in-person. For Christine Boatman, who teaches in the Estacada School District in Oregon, hybrid teaching during the summer of 2020 was an eye-opener.

For our district, the concept of a hybrid classroom involves some students coming to school in person and some students attending school via live-video technology, such as through Zoom. With the aid of Zoom, students who are online have the same access to the classroom as every student attending in person. . . .

FIG. 5.2. Primary-grade child learning arithmetic remotely (public domain).

The hybrid classroom includes a large web camera and high-quality speakers that allow the students connecting via Zoom to have a good view of the classroom, to hear everything the teacher is saying, and to be able to respond to the teacher and other classmates. The room also has a large television screen where the students who were Zooming in have their video feeds appear. Every student, both at home and in person, has a Chromebook where they complete the majority of their classwork. . . .

With the hybrid model, every student is able to get the same information presented by the teacher at the same time. Students are all given the same opportunity to participate in class discussions, to play whole-class games, and to participate in online-class activities. When I talked to a student about her experience in the hybrid class, she said, "It's really cool to have so much technology in my classroom, and I love that I can talk to my best friend, even if she's coming to school on Zoom instead of in person. . . ."

During the hybrid summer school program, one of the most exciting discoveries was that "kids Zooming in have been more engaged than in-person students," said math teacher Maria Warren. One of my students shared that she was so happy to see her friends again after being stuck at home for so long that she was paying close attention to everything that was happening in class.

In the hybrid classroom, all students are working on the same activities on Chromebooks. Students respond to discussion prompts in real time, teachers can cold-call on in-person students or students Zooming in, you can play online, whole-class games such as Kahoot!, and students can have great discussions about things they are learning about in class through Zoom breakout rooms. . . .

Through every student having their own Chromebook, the teacher can set up small groups of three to five students intermixed with in-person students and students Zooming in. This allows students to maintain relationships with their peers, as well as learn from them and practice valuable critical-thinking skills. . . . With instant messaging and discussion boards, there are many wonderful opportunities for students to share ideas and work together to solve problems. . . .

As we think about how to create the best possible experience for our students, teachers exploring hybrid classrooms will need to take risks, problem-solve, and try new things. Teachers will need to approach this work with patience and a growth mindset. The hybrid classroom provides a wonderful opportunity for teachers innovating to create a great environment for student learning.[8]

By March 2022, nearly all US teachers and students were back to face-to-face lessons in classrooms. Yet questions remain: How did teachers teach before schools closed their doors two years earlier? How have teachers taught since all students returned to classroom? While answering these questions is challenging, given the sparse data, I believe that previous chapters in this book offer strong clues to an answer.

For example, I have documented how schools over the past century have consistently depended upon the age-graded organization and how its grammar of instruction shaped to a degree how most teachers taught. Neither age-graded organization nor the grammar of instruction changed in schools across the nation during the pandemic.

Teachers, as other professionals do, create and rely upon routines. From positioning classroom furniture to taking attendance, administering tests, assigning homework, calling on students to answer questions, organizing small-group activities, and grading homework—teachers have routines. Assuredly, routines vary among teachers in the same school, but they nonetheless depend upon them to traverse lessons and get through the school day.[9]

Often these teacher-crafted routines reflect beliefs and experiences with how students learn, what are the best ways of teaching students with a range of academic differences, and how much time to devote to required curriculum standards and testing. Thus, teachers within the same elementary school vary in, say, how much time they devote to teaching math, reading and language arts, spelling, social studies and science. That variation also occurs district-wide. The history of the past century of teaching within the age-graded school and teachers' patterned routines driven by mind-sets and experiences indicate what was in place when Covid-19 struck in 2020.[10]

Moreover, in earlier chapters, I have described how teacher beliefs, class-room routines and experiences have created two fundamental traditions of teaching that capture the common ways teachers have taught their lessons: teacher- and student-centered instruction, and mixes of these traditions.

While the dominant teaching tradition since the closing decades of the nineteenth century has been teacher-centered, each generation of teachers since the 1920s has adopted the vocabulary and selected activities embedded in the student-centered tradition (e.g., focus on the whole child, learning by doing, small-group activities). Consequently, hybrids of these traditions have appeared again and again in widely different settings. Teacher-crafted blends of the two traditions, of course, account for variations across urban, subur-ban, rural, and exurban classrooms.[11]

When I focus on the years since 2005 but prior to the pandemic, surveys, case studies, teacher logs, and classroom observation completed in these years, few and limited as they are, largely support previous research on common pat-terns during the past century of classroom practice. While ways of teaching vary within and across schools in the same district—a pattern in of itself—it is well to keep in mind that classroom routines seldom turn on a dime.

Surveys and Studies, 2005–2020

I offer three studies of teaching practices, including meta-analyses from a mé-lange of research on classroom instruction that used surveys, collections of teacher logs, and in-depth case studies of specific teachers. Why these three? They focus on classroom instruction across elementary and secondary levels. They look within and across schools. They use both quantitative and qualita-tive methods. While there are assuredly other studies I might have included, these are suitable proxies for the very few published studies that examined classroom lessons during these years.

Primary Grade Writing Instruction. For their study of primary-grade writing instruction, researchers Laura Cutler and Steven Graham randomly sampled 178 primary-grade teachers who taught writing. They did this 2008 study because

> researchers currently have little data on what writing instruction looks like in schools. They do not have a good sense of how much students write or what they write. They also do not know how much time is devoted to writing in-struction; what writing skills, processes, or knowledge are taught to students; what methods are used to teach writing; how or even if technology is part of the writing program; or whether teachers assess students' writing progress. Without such information, it is difficult to determine what needs to be done.[12]

What they found in this national sample of primary-grade teachers who taught writing was great variability in the amount of time they taught writing and the balance between teaching discrete writing skills (basically a teacher-centered approach) and letting students write freely on topics they or the teacher chose (called "process writing"), or student-centered instruction.

Researchers concluded that

> the typical teacher placed considerable emphasis on teaching basic writing skills, as spelling, grammar, capitalization, and punctuation skills were reportedly taught daily, with handwriting and sentence construction skills taught several times a week. The typical teacher also reported using a variety of practices common to the process writing approach. This included having students plan (at least weekly) and revise their compositions (at least several times a month), conference with and help other students with their writing (at least several times a month), share their writing with classmates (at least weekly), monitor their writing progress (at least weekly), choose their own writing topics (at least half the time), work at their own pace (at least half of the time), and use invented spellings (most of the time).[13]

As to the writing activities, teachers said that primary students were writing stories (96 percent), drawing pictures and writing something to go with them (95 percent), writing letters to another person (89 percent), writing journals (86 percent), and using worksheets (86 percent).[14] Teachers reported that most of their instruction was done in whole groups (56 percent), with 23 percent done through small-group activities).[15]

The researchers concluded that "most primary grade teachers take an eclectic approach to writing instruction, combining elements from the two most common methods for teaching writing: process writing and skills instruction (although they generally place less emphasis on process writing). In addition, almost all teachers reported using most of the practices surveyed, but there was considerable variability between teachers in how often they applied each practice."[16]

Mid-Continent Research for Education and Learning (2005). In the wake of No Child Left Behind legislation (2001), which called for US schools and teachers to embrace state and subject matter curriculum standards in math and science in order to get US students to reach higher levels of academic achievement, McREL did a meta-analysis of 113 studies that met their research criteria on the impact of curriculum standards upon teacher instruction and student achievement in math and science.[17] For example, McREL wanted to find out whether teachers adopted and used the recommended teaching practices of the inquiry-driven curriculum of the National Council of Teachers of

Math, published just prior to the passage of the federally funded No Child Left Behind Act.

The standards of the National Council of Teachers of Mathematics (NCTM) aimed to shift the direction of math teaching from traditional teacher-directed instruction that focused on memorizing rules and doing problem-sets in math textbooks to student-centered practices that encouraged teachers to ask tougher kinds of questions and get students to analyze and explain math operations. NCTM standards promoted classroom activities where students collaborated in solving real-world problems while understanding and using basic math concepts.

Based upon their review, McREL researchers concluded that

standards-based curricula can change teacher instruction, although eight of the 15 studies presented mixed results on this outcome. Positive findings indicated that standards-based curricula can motivate and help teachers to change their pedagogy so it more closely reflects the recommendations of the NCTM. Teachers using these curricula were more likely to have students explain their answers, allow for multiple solutions to problems, incorporate more problem-solving activities into their classrooms, use more pair work, and spend less class time on presentation and whole-group work than teachers using traditional curricula.

On the other hand, a notable finding is that many teachers expressed knowledge about NCTM-oriented practices but struggled with using them in their classroom. Some teachers also said that they experienced more stress and increased preparation time when implementing standards and standards-based curricula, compared with traditional curricula. Finally, implementation of a standards-based curriculum alone did not influence changes in teachers' instruction unless student assessments and textbooks were aligned with that curriculum—indicating that systemic support is important for changing pedagogical practice.[18]

As with previous efforts since the 1980s to get teachers to adopt new curriculum standards, the new math standards of the early 2000s, working within the federally driven framework of No Child Left Behind, achieved mixed results when it came to altering routine teacher-centered instruction. Changes in daily classroom practices depended wholly on whether districts and schools established teacher-friendly structures that would guide and help teachers in implementing the standards partially, moderately, or completely.

Studying Reading Instruction with Teacher Logs. In 2009, researchers Brian Rowan and Richard Correnti published an article drawn from their study of 75,000 teacher logs from 1,945 elementary school teachers who taught reading in 112 schools across the United States. After analyzing their logs and going through the literature on new reading research and existing state and national standards for teaching reading, the researchers concluded that

> the average first-grade teacher . . . provided teacher-directed instruction in reading comprehension about 70% of days; but about 16% of first-grade teachers taught like this on fewer than 40% of days, whereas another 84% did so on nearly 90% of all days.
>
> Similarly, the average first-grade teacher . . . had students discuss texts with other students on about 30% of days when reading comprehension was taught; but teachers 1 standard deviation below the mean in this same (average) school had students discuss texts with each other on only 16% of days, whereas teachers 1 standard deviation above the mean had students discuss texts nearly 70% of days.
>
> This wide variability among teachers at the same grade in the same school holds for a wide range of teaching practices, not only in reading comprehension but also in writing and word analysis, demonstrating once again just how important a student's location in a particular classroom within a school is to that student's opportunity to learn to read.[19]

These three studies of teaching writing, math, and reading—all within age-graded schools—illustrate anew the common patterns of teaching that have been around for nearly a century: although teacher-directed instruction dominates classroom lessons, hybrids of it that include some student-centered instruction are ever-present as well. Variation in lessons is a common feature of the hybrids of two traditions of teaching that have evolved over the past century within US schools.

New curriculum standards and district requirements about teaching methods do influence classroom practices marginally. The degree of influence depends on the willingness of the district and school to marshal resources and build mechanisms to help teachers apply top-down policies to daily lessons. Teachers, of course, ultimately decide what to adopt and what to ignore as policies change. Hybrid practices expand, and researchers (as well as policymakers and practitioners) continue to comment on how three algebra teachers located in the same high school, for example, spend different amounts of time on equations, diverge in organizing student grouping for the lesson, and vary in their use of worksheets, textbooks, and other materials.

Furthermore, these three studies underscore the realities of classroom research in US schools. First, the dependence upon surveys. Because of the high cost and labor-intensiveness of observational studies of classrooms—the gold standard of classroom research—most investigators turn to surveys, teacher logs, and interviews to find out what happens as lessons unfold. Second, within these century-old traditions of teaching and their hybrids, clear variations existed within the same grade and subject, within the same school, and across district schools in how teachers organized lessons, what they taught, how long they taught it.

Even though states and districts map out what content and skills teachers are expected to teach at each grade level; even though parents, teachers, and students accept annual, weekly, and daily schedules in elementary and secondary schools; and even though teachers remain responsible for the health, safety, and learning of students, two research-driven conclusions are consistent for these years. First, teacher-directed instruction, with a smattering of student-directed activities, governs most lessons. Second, great variability in teaching due to teacher-crafted hybrids exists in how teachers enact these century-old traditions of teaching within the age-graded school. Both stability and change are constant. Such constancy in organization, rules, and classroom practice is hardly novel. That stability has come to include many changes, particularly in the adoption of technologies in and out of school, even in the brief, fifteen-year period that I consider here.

Though past teaching practices cannot exactly predict present ones, since social, political, and economic changes periodically sweep across American society, and student demography and the annual attrition rate of teachers affect what occurs in US schools, patterns of stability in teaching practices persist. Moreover, the increasing use of new technologies and changes in public school governance (i.e., charters), plus the incremental changes described earlier in school organization and classroom practices, have rattled but not altered age-graded school structures. The grammar of schooling remains remarkably stable amid many teacher-crafted, incremental changes.[20] Therefore, readers do not need piles of new data as we examine recent schooling and classroom practices, given the history I have detailed in this book.

Certainly, the recent pandemic has affected three academic years, and it remains dicey to claim without offering some evidence that teaching methods used since 2005 have persisted after the arrival of Covid-19 in 2020. I therefore take a brief look at what evidence I have gathered about teaching during the pandemic.

Teaching during Covid-19

Descriptions of classroom lessons evoke a partial picture of more continuity than change in how teachers present daily content and skills to their students. A few teachers have described their remote and in-person lessons during and after school closures. Here is an account from brand-new teacher, D'Lanie Pelletier at E. O. Smith High School in Mansfield, Connecticut:

This year has brought students in masks with shields over their desks, hybrid learning, block schedules, fully online students, and the struggle to keep students engaged despite the uncertainty of their outside world. All of the teaching and classroom management strategies that I learned in my teacher preparation program now seemed distant as all teachers learned how to adapt and teach in this new learning model. . . .

I went into the first week nervous and unsure of how the lessons were going to unfold. Through many trials and errors, I have found new ways to connect with and engage my students, some of whom I have never even met in person. Applications such as Nearpod, Edpuzzle, Kahoot!, and Quizlet Live have become an integral part of my lessons. I have found that these apps keep the students, whether at home or in person, engaged and participating in the classwork.

Another quality that I have learned in my first year is [*sic*] patience and compassion. Just as many adults are tired and struggling this year, our students are feeling this same way. They are behind screens all day and are unable to hang out with their friends as they could years before. Sometimes as teachers, we forget that our students can feel the same burnout and exhaustion that we feel. I learned that being patient with students and showing them that you understand can go a long way. . . .

As a first-year teacher, I often feel as if I have to prove myself. I want to prove to my students, colleagues, and the administration that I am capable of this job. However, this led to a massive amount of overthinking and stress that wasn't good for me or my students' learning. I had to see that it is OK to make mistakes. . . .[21]

Laura Estes-Swilley, a high school English teacher for twenty-one years, recounts her feelings and experiences after she returned to face-to-face instruction in 2020 at Durant High School in Hillsborough County, Florida.

Our students have the choice between e-learning and attending brick-and-mortar schools. I am teaching in the classroom, but many of my peers are teaching e-learning from home and some are teaching a few online classes from their empty classrooms.

Then there are those teaching classes in person and online synchronously, with 50 or 60 students per period. Those teaching from home feel cut off, and in many ways they are. The teachers juggling in-person and online students at the same time are overwhelmed to a level I've never seen. They feel misused, because they are. There is a splintering. That's natural, because everyone is struggling, but it's not helping morale.

Gone are the days of lunching with our peers, talking about our days or what works with a specific kid or lesson or text. Gone are the days of just sharing our lives with each other. Teaching has always been isolating; we are almost always apart from each other. Our lives are filled with kids and that's the best part of teaching, but sometimes we need adult voices. There are few now. . . .

I have 130 students and what kept me awake this summer was not knowing if I would be able protect them. I had not yet met them, but I knew how important they were. I had never experienced fear at Durant High School until Aug. 31, the first day of school. Some of my fear was unfounded. We are all adjusting to the misery of day-long masking; we are cleaning desks between every class; we don't share supplies or books. We have had, to date, only two student cases of the coronavirus, but we have over 30 students quarantined. . . .

I find the most painful thing is the one for which I haven't prepared. It hit when I checked my messages and read "re: COVID sucks." It was only the second week of school and already one of my seniors was letting me know he would have to quarantine. I realized this was going to happen again, again and probably again, until it began to feel normal. I'm so tired of the phrase "the new normal."

My heart dropped into my stomach reading the message from that student, who is in one of my AP Literature classes. I soon began my own version of synchronous teaching as he Zoomed into class daily to join our discussions. I am lucky to have such dedicated students, but when I read that message, I wasn't thinking about curricular concerns. I was worried and I was sad; I hardly knew him, but I wanted better for him. I want better for all of them. . . .

When I consider these students I have only known for a month, I feel incredibly hopeful. They are resilient. They sanitize; they wear masks without complaint; they sit six feet apart at lunch; they embrace the opportunity to be in school; they are planning for the future; they are excited to start their adult lives. In short, they are beautiful. And I am lucky to know them.[22]

For the Covid-19 years, I could not find research studies that used surveys, collected teacher logs, or depended upon classroom observations. So I relied upon journalists and firsthand accounts since the pandemic arrived. What these few teacher accounts tell me is that the natural disaster of a pandemic has surely altered "normal" schooling across the nation's thousands of districts, with sudden closures, the need to re-organize for remote instruction, and a gradual reopening of classrooms.

With surges of infections from mutations in the coronavirus (e.g., Delta, Omicron) throughout the winter of 2021–2022, some district officials closed schools (e.g., Chicago), while other district leaders kept them open (e.g., New York). Staff shortages, including a shrinking pool of substitute teachers, due to exposure to the virus created a hopscotch of openings and closings across the country. The commitment to keeping schools open, however, remained strong. By the beginning of 2022, schooling, and daily life have returned to some version of "normal."[23]

From the limited evidence I have seen, the closing and opening of schools over the past three years have not at all shifted the dominant teacher-centered approach and its hybrids to more student-centered forms of instruction or transformed daily lessons in ways that would send progressive cheerleaders into spasms of joy. Hybrids do persist, even in the teacher accounts I have included. Classroom furniture arrangements remained as before. Lessons planned prior to school closures were taken out of folders and used. Teachers scheduled small-group activities. Teacher talk continued to outstrip student talk, as it had before Covid-19. The "new normal" was basically an adaptation to what had been occurring in schools and classrooms before the pandemic, except for masks, physical distancing, increased ventilation, and frequent sanitizing of school and classroom surfaces.

Even with 65 percent of American adults fully vaccinated (but less among teachers and students), Covid-19 and its variants by March 2022 had reshaped how Americans interact with one another while pumping up anxieties about interacting with unvaccinated friends and strangers.[24] But in schools, the age-graded organization and its grammar of schooling chugged along unperturbed by surges of infections from Delta and Omicron mutations.

So What?

The answer to this chapter's question, How do teachers teach now? is transparent. Historic patterns of classroom practice in US age-graded schools over the past century, counting incremental changes, have persisted between 2005–2022, even with the arrival and protracted presence of a virus that had initially shut down most of the nation's schools. Schools reopened during the pandemic and will continue to welcome students and staff as the virus becomes endemic.

While some pundits and policymakers have called for major reforms in schooling after the emergency shutdown (e.g., extending remote instruction, adding staff to help with mental health of students), most administrators, teachers, and parents wanted schools to return to what existed before March 2020. And that appears to be the case when it comes to documenting how teachers taught in the past two decades.[25]

The two traditions of teaching and their myriad mixes have persevered in US schools over the past century. Earlier chapters on how teachers taught, the slow accumulation of incremental changes in schooling and teaching, and overall stability in teaching suggest that amid constancy in teaching practices, reformers then and now continue to press for schools to be more student-driven and teaching practice to be more student-directed. Or, as one scholar recently said, "COVID-19 provides the right opportunity for all schools to try to change the how of learning. Teachers and schools could start with a few questions: Do we need to teach all the time, given that so many online teaching resources are already available? Can we start learning by asking students to identify a problem they wish to solve and helping them find solutions? Is it possible for students to learn without us teaching them?"[26]

The existence of teaching hybrids and great variation in how teachers teach is strong evidence of a blending of two teaching traditions. Each generation of policy-driven reformers, university scholars, administrators, and practitioners imbued with notions of individualized instruction, student collaboration, opening up schools to the world outside, and, yes, learning by doing, presses for student-centered curricula and instruction that achieve these outcomes. Yet the existing policy regime anchored in state and district standards, tests, and political accountability insures that all students who wish to go to college or enter a career upon high school graduation will do so. And, I must add, these dedicated reformers seldom, if at all, mention the century-old structure of the age-graded school as a target for reform.

The historic contradictions between reformers' demands for more student-centered teaching and equally fervent crusaders who call for maintaining tough curriculum standards, standardized tests, and political accountability are painfully obvious. They need to be parsed and connected to previous chapters on stability and change in classroom practice. The next chapter seeks to do both.

Why Have Changing and Conserving Been Hallmarks of US Public Schooling and Teaching Practice?

Teachers at Garfield High School in the LAUSD (Los Angeles Unified School District) were winding down classes for the approaching lunch break when they heard the startling sound of people—they were not sure who—running through the halls, pounding on classroom doors. "Walkout!" they were shouting. "Walkout!"

They looked on in disbelief as hundreds of students streamed out of classrooms and assembled before the school entrance, their clenched fists held high. "Viva la revolución!" they called out. "Education, not eradication!" Soon, sheriff's deputies were rumbling in.

It was just past noon on a sunny Tuesday, March 5, 1968—the day a Mexican American revolution began. Soon came walkouts at two more Eastside high schools, Roosevelt and Lincoln, in protest of run-down campuses, lack of college prep courses, and teachers who were poorly trained, indifferent, or racist.

By the time the "blowouts" peaked about a week later, 22,000 students had stormed out of class, delivered impassioned speeches, and clashed with police. Scenes of rebellion filled newspapers and television screens. School trustees held emergency meetings to try to quell the crisis; Mayor Sam Yorty suggested students had fallen under the influence of "communist agitators."

What these Mexican American students did in 1968, of course, did not occur in a vacuum. It occurred at a time when black students, teachers, and civil rights activists in the South—recall Mississippi's Freedom Schools in 1964— were also taking matters into their own hands to improve both the schooling and traditional teaching practices they experienced.

The contemporary civil rights movement that had initially begun in the mid-1950s South flowered across the United States in the following decades. In California, a drive to mobilize young Mexican Americans (or Chicanos, a popular, racially aware word at the time), to exert their rights and improve their lives in the segregated barrios in which they lived, the jobs they were hired for, and the schools they attended had already begun in the early 1960s. Recall, for example, that César Chávez and Dolores Huerta had founded the United Farm Workers union during the 1965 strike of grape pickers; also court cases challenging segregated Mexican American schools were wending their way through federal court.[1]

The "blowouts," then, occurred within the context of the larger civil rights movement roiling all public institutions that had practiced segregation, including schools. What these Mexican American students and teachers wanted in 1968 was much-improved schooling, including teachers who were far more engaged in teaching content and skills, instead of what they were then experiencing in understaffed, overcrowded, poorly maintained buildings where their daily lessons were disconnected from their lives. They sought an education that better reflected who they were and wanted to be.[2]

Consider the following excerpts from the demands that these Latin students and teachers submitted to LAUSD authorities:

- Bilingual, Bi-cultural education will be compulsory for Mexican Americans in the Los Angeles City School System where there is a majority of Mexican-American students. This program will be open to all other students on a voluntary basis. . . . In-service education programs will be instituted immediately for all staff in order to teach them the Spanish language and increase their understanding of the history, traditions, and contributions of the Mexican culture. . . .
- Administrators and teachers who show any form of prejudice toward Mexican or Mexican American students, including failure to recognize, understand, and appreciate Mexican culture and heritage, will be removed from East Los Angeles schools. . . .
- Textbooks and curriculum will be developed to show Mexican and Mexican American contributions to the U.S. society and to show the injustices that Mexicans have suffered as a culture of that society. Textbooks should concentrate on Mexican folklore rather than English folklore.
- All administrators where schools have a majority of Mexican American descent shall be of Mexican American descent. If necessary, training programs should be instituted to provide a cadre of Mexican American administrators.[3]

Note, however, that the dominant mode of instruction—teacher-centered instruction—was not mentioned in the students' demands. It was not part of the list of reformist demands propelling the students' walkout. How teachers taught daily in these high schools was taken for granted, as were the rows of desks facing the blackboard in each classroom, using textbooks, and taking tests. In short, like most school reform, changes occurred in curriculum and hiring of bilingual teachers, but the prevailing mode of classroom teaching continued.

So what did city authorities and Los Angeles Unified School District policymakers do in response to these demands after walkouts that shut down the city's high schools? The city's reaction was swift:

> Law enforcement responded with undercover operations, raids and arrests. In June, authorities rounded up 13 activists, who were indicted by a grand jury on charges including conspiracy in having planned the walkouts. Each faced 66 years in prison.
>
> Among those indicted were [David] Sanchez, [founder of the Brown Berets] and Sal Castro, who was the only teacher to publicly participate and back students' complaints to news media and school district officials.
>
> He lost his job but was eventually reinstated after months of protests by Eastside parents. Castro had employment, but was bounced around to different campuses and made a substitute before finally landing at Belmont as a teacher. The indictments against the "Eastside 13" were struck down by an appeals court in 1970.[4]

As for the LAUSD School Board, it immediately accepted two of the demands for more bilingual faculty/administration and smaller classes. As to the other demands, the Board of Education said they were already working on what the students wanted (e.g., curriculum materials) or that they lacked the funds to comply.

Teacher-Inspired Reform

Articles on the walkout often mentioned the role that Sal Castro, a Lincoln High School social studies teacher, played in organizing students to leave school. As one history of the protest put it, "Sal Castro, through his idealism, commitment, and courage, made history. He is not a victim of history but a maker of history. It is a story of the role of the individual in history. Sal's story reminds us that people make history and that one individual can make a difference."[5] Keep in mind that before Castro became a high school social studies teacher, he attended Los Angeles Community College and had gone to annual meetings of the Chicano Youth Leadership Conferences, a network of Mexican American activists. These activists began meeting in 1963, and Castro became part of that network when LAUSD hired him. He continued to work with college and high school students, educating them to the inequalities they endured, helping them draw up demands backed up with evidence of inadequate resources in barrio schools, unequal facilities, and the lack of bilingual teachers and curricular content that included Mexican history and immigration. All of these experiences prepared Castro, his students, and network activists for what happened in 1968.[6]

Now reconsider the concessions the LAUSD Board of Education granted to protesting teachers and students after the walkout. In effect, the board agreed to changes that ended up both reforming and conserving LAUSD high schools, including existing teaching practices. How can that be? More bilingual teachers were hired. New curriculum content featuring Mexican Americans appeared. Yet teaching practices largely remained the same. School authorities accepted the changes that students and teachers demanded but avoided alterations in how teachers taught. Then they reopened those closed East L. A. high schools, thereby restoring political stability to the district.

The 1968 walkout, then, was not about changing how teachers taught in these largely Mexican American high schools. It was about the lack of Mexican history in social studies courses; it was about introducing bilingual instruction; it was about hiring more Mexican American teachers and appointing principals of that ethnicity. How teachers taught, the prevailing teacher-centered instruction, was absent from the list of demands. That is the conserving part of school reform, another instance of dynamic conservatism in action. Now, nearly a half-century later, there is a new charter school in the LAUSD named Sal Castro Middle School.[7]

The dynamic conservatism revealed in the LAUSD during and after the 1968 walkouts is fundamental to how educational systems work in America and is reflected in other urban districts, schools, and classrooms. Consider the following prime example of the charter school movement.

Charter School-Inspired Reform and Stability in Classroom Practice

Since 1991, when Minnesota became the first state to charter new schools free of most education regulations, forty-four states and the District of Columbia have authorized 7,700 charter schools run by nonprofit and for-profit organizations. As of 2020, charters enrolled over three million students, or just over 7 percent of US public school enrollment.[8]

Free of many state regulations, these charters are public schools governed by independent boards of parents, teachers, university professors, community members, entrepreneurs, and so forth. Charters receive state funds for each student equal to what a regular public school next door would receive. They are open to all students in a district, and students are usually chosen by lottery. These new and largely autonomous organizations are accountable to their boards (not the elected school board of the district in which they are located) to fulfill the aims stipulated in the charter they received.[9]

The theory behind charter schools that drove nearly all states to establish them was that such schools would be free to innovate in how they would organize a school, create a curriculum, and develop engaging lessons for children and youth. That freedom to innovate would lead to different ways of schooling that would prod regular public schools to alter their traditional organization and approaches to delivering classroom lessons. That's the theory.[10]

Between the theory and the realities that were charter schools across the nation, succeeding decades saw the unfolding of a range of charters that encompassed the very best and the very worst of schools. Most ended up in the middle, quite like regular public schools in organization, curriculum, and, yes, teaching practices.

Going from zero to 7 percent of total US students in charter schools in thirty years isn't as quick a move as a cat video going viral in hours on social media but in institutional terms it is a solid sign that charter schools have become part of daily scene in US public schools and are here to stay. Publicly funded charter schools have found a special niche within urban districts. Fifty-eight percent of all charters are in cities; the rest are in suburban and rural districts, many of which are poor.[11] Two-thirds of charter school students are minority (across the country, the percentage is 50 percent).

Currently, urban districts with high percentages of students attending charter schools are New Orleans (99.6), San Antonio (50.2), Gary, Indiana (50.1), Kansas City, Missouri (46.1), and Washington, DC (43.1). Charters expanded parental choice beyond magnet schools and alternative schools, giving districts portfolios of options. Charters have become as familiar as the morning Pledge of Allegiance in the nation's urban classrooms.[12]

Major foundations such as Walton, Gates, Broad, and the Doris and Donald Fisher Fund have donated hundreds of millions to promote charter schools. Donors see charters as a way of ridding the nation (especially big city schools) of an obsolete model of schooling that fails to prepare US youth for either college or an ever-changing workplace. Foundation officials, many urban parent groups, and civic and business leaders have supported the expansion of charter management organizations and independent charters. Opponents have been teacher unions, groups of parents railing at loss of funds for regular public schools, and other groups who see a lack of accountability in dumping fiscally and academically failing charters.[13]

Warring research studies from camps promoting and opposing charters have argued for the past three decades whether charters are academically outperforming traditional public schools. It has become a trivial question, however, because there is so such diversity among charter schools. Some charters (e.g., KIPP and Summit Schools) send nearly all graduates to college; others go out of business; some charters are for-profit, such as cyber schools. Lumping them all together to answer a generic question—which form of public schools is better academically?—is not only goofy but also fruitless. What is clear, however, after thirty years is a lack of systemic oversight and accountability of charters for poor fiscal and academic performance in various states.[14] What is also clear is that the promised autonomy for charter schools to become innovative in curriculum and instruction, part of the original mandate for charters, has yet to materialize in these schools and classrooms.[15]

Is Teaching in Charter Schools Better, Worse, or the Same as in Regular Schools?

What has become obvious in this thirty-year history is that elementary and secondary charter schools have far greater flexibility than regular district schools in altering what happens in classrooms and buildings (think of charter school organizations that have built unique school cultures, such as KIPP and Aspire). Yet even with that mandate of separate governance and the charge to innovate in both organization and instruction, most charter schools have replicated the traditional age-graded arrangement. Ditto for the curriculum, since accreditation, which is a must for any newly organized school, requires conforming to state standards for curriculum and skills that must be taught.[16]

Does that replication of regular school organization and curriculum extend to teaching practices? Does teaching in a charter school, with its separate governance and organizational flexibility harnessed to a mission to innovate, differ at all from teaching in a noncharter school? I have observed dozens of charter school classrooms over the past decade. I have seen extraordinary, ordinary, and a few disastrous lessons. Consider Katie Goddard, who in 2016 taught world history at one of the Summit Charter high schools in the San Francisco Bay Area.

The young, slim teacher stands on the chair in the middle of the classroom to be heard above ninth-grade students clustered in the four corners of the portable classroom. The students are chattering about the reasons they agree or disagree with the statement Katie Goddard, the teacher, put on the "smart board." The statement students considered—"There is no single group responsible for the crime of slavery. African rulers are equally as guilty for slavery"—drove them to different corners labeled "strongly agree," "agree," "disagree," "strongly disagree." The teacher asks students in each corner why they agree or disagree with statement. After a few students give their reasons, some classmates change their minds and migrate to different corners, making the classroom a swirl of movement. This activity occurred in the middle of a ninety-five-minute block in World Studies where Goddard was introducing a new unit on Imperialism.

Goddard had begun the class with a Warm-Up question: "Should the U.S. pay reparations to black Americans whose families have been slaves?" After telling them to put away their cells and Chromebooks, she gave them two short op-ed pieces on opposite sides of the question. One piece argued that who should pay and who should receive reparations for enslaving Africans were contested and confused. The other argued that the British should pay reparations to Kenyans for what they did in colonizing that African nation.

She asks the twenty-four ninth-graders to "read and chunk the text" for each opinion piece. She reminded the class to read each paragraph and write a one-line summary of each paragraph and indicate whether they agreed or disagreed. As students write in their notebooks, Goddard, holding a clipboard, walks around the classroom of 13 tables, each seating two students facing the "smart board," answering questions, and checking to see what students are writing. Goddard asks students to hold up fingers indicating how much more time they want to finish task. Some hold up one, others two and three. For those who had finished she offers two options for them to do.

She then asks students to share with partners their summaries and opinions. As students start talking to one another, Goddard interrupts and says, "Remember in working together you need to turn to your partner, move your body to face one another, and listen carefully to what your partner says." Students resume talking.

When she sees that nearly all students have completed the task, she asks them for their summaries of the two articles and which one they agree/disagree with most. Students are initially reluctant to commit to a position, but as a few offer their opinions, Goddard teases out the reasons embedded in arguments for and against reparations. And this is the moment when the teacher asked all the students to take a position on the statement and go to a corner of the room: "There is no single group responsible for the crime of slavery. African rulers are equally as guilty for slavery."

This Warm-Up and debate about reparations were initial activities in the lesson introducing Imperialism. Starting with the contentious contemporary question of reparations for slavery, Goddard would move to instances of European countries colonizing the Congo in Africa and India, and in Asia in the nineteenth and twentieth centuries and consider the human costs of taking over these countries.

The agenda for the day, written on the whiteboard, listed the sequence of topics for the hour-and-a-half session:

1. Reparations
2. Slavery op-eds
3. Criteria
4. Imperialism op-eds
5. Exit ticket

After the Warm-Up and during the four-corner debate, Goddard gets deeper into the reparations question by introducing statements such as, "slavery ended a hundred years ago, so the U.S. government should not pay any money to African Americans now." One student points out that the US government has already paid reparations when they gave sums of money to Japanese Americans for being in internment camps during World War II. Another points out that the money went to those who were still alive. Voices are raised and tone becomes adversarial among students agreeing and disagreeing. Goddard interrupts and says, "Remember our norms. The second your tone becomes combative, you don't listen. Our goal is to listen to one another." After more restrained back-and-forth in which the teacher specifically calls on students who have heretofore not entered the discussion, Goddard asks class if they want to shift corners.

About one-third of the students move to another corner.

Teacher now asks students to return to their tables and turn to the next question: When are reparations necessary? She asks class to open Chromebooks and come up with criteria to answer the question. She reminds class that there is no correct answer, that you have different opinions but you need examples and facts to support your opinion. Goddard moves around the room asking and answering questions at each table.

After about ten minutes, Goddard asks students to put lids of laptops down and says that "we are going to study Imperialism and you are going to write an op-ed by the end of the unit. The question you will answer," she says, is "do former imperializing countries have a responsibility to give foreign aid to the countries they imperialized?" She links the earlier discussion of reparations to Imperialism and then previews the next twelve lessons on the "smart board," going over each one briefly. She then puts up a slide that defines Imperialism as "the process of taking over another country through diplomacy or military force." Goddard asks students to come up with their definition of imperialism by using Playlist of sources (documents and videos)—she gives the class the link—that she assembled for them on the Congo, India, and other colonized countries. She urges students to talk to their partners in coming up with their definitions. After pairs have come up with their definitions from Playlist, she asks them to brainstorm what they would need to know about imperialism to determine if reparations are necessary.

With clipboard in hand, teacher moves through the classroom checking to see which students are unclear about the task or having difficulties in answering questions.

As time winds down to end the class, Goddard summarizes what they have done, connecting discussions on reparations to new unit of Imperialism.

These are the criteria I use in judging the quality of a lesson: clear and coherent organization, presence of mixed activities, frequent verbal interaction between teacher and students and among students, and, finally, a summary of the lesson.[17] In my opinion, Goddard's lesson met these criteria fully. As I left this charter school lesson in world history, I was thoroughly impressed with what I saw and experienced.

In the same year, I also observed a math classroom at another charter school. Here is what I recorded in my notes.

The Precalculus class began at 10:40 and ended at 12:15. Ethan Edwards is in his third year of teaching. He was a math major at University of California, Santa Cruz, and got his credential to teach at the University of California, Davis, before coming to this charter school. He, like other teachers at his school who have been there at least one year, floats to different classrooms in the building; first-year teachers have one classroom the entire day. So at the beginning of the block 2 class, he and a few students are shoving tables into rows facing the front to get ready for his class. Four tables sitting two students each in three rows accommodated the twenty-four students who arrived. As in all Summit classrooms, there was an LCD projector and screen at front of room that showed slides as the teacher clicked keys.

The agenda for the day is on the screen.

- Warm-Up Analysis
- Essay Overview
- Independent work time + workshop
- Goal: finish paragraph
- Reflection

Since the class will be visiting University of California, Davis for the next two days, Edwards flashes slides of buildings at Davis that they will see. He asked students to turn in forms for the trip later in the day. He explains the housing arrangements—four students to a room. There were ripples of excitement and nervousness about the trip, especially after he announced that there will be four students to each car in driving to Davis. Students look around, start signaling one another to share same car. Edwards says: "I can feel the tension in the room over who I will be with for the trip." That lowers the murmuring and tension. There were a few questions from students. He reassures students by saying that it is a short trip to the university. Teacher then segues to lesson.

"I want to talk about how we are going to predict tuition increases through 2020 from the data set I gave you. We will be doing scatter plots and writing different regression equations." Edwards proceeds to explain the making of regression curves (linear, exponential, and polynomial)—the central point of the lesson—using the whiteboard as he writes down these concepts. He goes over "key features" of such data and equations and how they get displayed as outliers, intercepts, slope, rate of growth, and residuals. In every instance, he defines them and brings into the explanation particular students who respond to his choral questions (these are questions directed to the entire class and have no student name attached either before or after the question is asked). Students do contribute. Teacher draws on the whiteboard examples of each concept thereby defining the terms for class. He brings the explanation of what students will work on to a close, saying, "So, I just talked a lot about some high level stuff." He asks, "Are there any questions?" No one asks a question.

Teacher then turns to spreadsheet of data on tuition costs for two colleges. "So you are going to look at how to use this spreadsheet to come up with functions to predict increases in tuition costs through 2020." He passes out data sets and asks students to pair with partner to go through the data.

Before students open their Chromebooks to look at spreadsheets and begin work, Edwards goes over with whole group, step-by-step, how they are to create a linear regression equation. Does same for exponential and then polynomial equations. During his explanation, he asks choral questions of class to check for understanding. A few students respond to each query. When hearing one or two responses that match the question, he picks an answer and continues the explanation. After he finishes going over the three regression equations, he asks: "Are there any questions about how to use the data spreadsheet to create these equations?"

No student asks a question.

He returns to explaining where students should input data. He then directs students to open their Chromebooks.

"I am going to give you guys thirty minutes to start to work in pairs on spreadsheet to make proper equations." He discusses due date for when they will turn in their work.

For next thirty minutes Edwards moves up and down aisles to answer questions, check on what each student is doing, and help individual students who are having trouble with task. At this point I left the classroom because of another appointment.

Referring back to the criteria I used in judging the quality of a social studies lesson: Was there a clear and coherent organization? Were there mixes of activities over the course of the lesson? To what degree were there verbal exchanges between teacher and students and among students? And finally, was there a summary of the lesson? Except for the final two criteria, I judged the math lesson to have met the standards satisfactorily.[18]

How typical are these two lessons of charter school teaching? Reviewing studies of charter school teaching over the years, I do believe they are typical of the range of lessons I have observed. Were there awful lessons (e.g., teacher lost control of the students during the lesson, the academic content of the lesson was well below what students could achieve, much incoherence in flow of lesson)? While I did see a few such lessons, overall, the frequency of competent teaching that I observed was about the same as I have seen in noncharter classrooms.

Keep in mind, however, that while the teaching loads of charter school teachers and noncharter teachers are similar, charter teachers have a much larger band of autonomy in which to create lessons, gather resources, and put them into practice in their classrooms. That increased discretion available to charter teachers surely appeared in some instances but, overall, given my limited observations, less than I would have expected.

What evidence is there beyond my observations that with even more teacher autonomy and flexibility in charter schools there is little difference between their classroom practices and those of their peers in public schools? To answer this question, I turn to researchers who examined studies of pedagogy across charter and noncharter schools.

One study concluded that "charter schoolteachers do not indicate higher levels of academic focus on learning. What we did find, however, is that in-school organizational conditions, conditions often attributed to effective schools, such as professional community and principal leadership, are associated with higher levels of academic focus. Furthermore, charter schools were not more likely than regular public schools to exhibit these in -school organizational conditions."[19] Such findings leave big holes in the ambitious theory that launched charter schools. Like their counterparts in regular public schools, charter school teachers mainly use a range of teacher-centered classroom practices such as lectures, scripted lessons, textbooks, worksheets, and homework often seasoned by certain student-centered practices, such as small-group work, student discussions, project-based learning, internships, and independent learning.

Keep in mind that when I use the phrases "teacher-centered" and "student-centered" instruction, I do not claim that such teaching practices are either appropriate or inappropriate, effective or ineffective with students. I am reporting what many researchers, including myself, have documented in classrooms. Yet the careful reader will have noted in earlier chapters that I do favor hybrids combining both traditions of teaching, constrained as they are by the age-graded school organization. That is my bias. That bias, however, keeps me aware of the importance of reporting accurately and documenting fully how teachers have taught and do teach now in regular and charter public schools.

Consider, for example, the Knowledge Is Power Program (KIPP). Its 255 elementary and secondary schools that serve over 112,000 students are age-graded charters where parents choose to send their children. Teaching approaches are unmistakably teacher-centered, although many KIPP teachers have incorporated student-centered tactics.[20] KIPP is not, of course, representative of all charter schools in its teaching practices. Aspire, Green Dot, and other charter management organizations have schools in their networks where hybrids of teaching practices are more evident but still operate within the tradition of teacher-centeredness.

Note that these elementary and secondary school charter schools are geared to preparing children and youth for college. That is their unvarnished mission. College prep begins early in these charter elementary and secondary schools; frontal teaching, direct instruction, extended day, and no-nonsense approaches to student behavior are the norm. Any variation among teachers in different networks of charter schools falls within a narrow band of teacher-centered practices—again, when I use that phrase, I do not suggest that such practices are inappropriate or ineffective. Teaching practices in charters and public schools appear more similar than different from one another, but as more evidence from direct observation of lessons becomes available, that view may change.

Since the mid-1990s, then, charter schools, freed from the constraints of state regulation and primed to be innovative in organization, curriculum, and instruction, have become an established part of the US landscape of tax-supported public schooling in cities and suburbs. By expanding parental choice beyond the neighborhood school, charter schools have succeeded in enrolling 7 percent of the nation's students. After three decades, they are clearly here to stay. Yet, given the available evidence, in organization, curriculum, and classroom practice they often resemble the public schools that that they were expected to outstrip. Consider what has occurred in Oakland Unified School District in the San Francisco Bay Area.

Oakland Unified School District:
Embracing and Expanding Charter Schools Amid Fiscal
Mismanagement and Shrinking Enrollments

While charters are public schools and receive state funds, district boards of education have one pot of money; each district draws up a budget that allocates sums to charters and regular schools. Monies that go to charters, then, mean fewer dollars go to a district's noncharter schools. If enrollments increase, states send more money to districts. However, if the number of students in a district shrinks, states send fewer dollars, which means that both charters and regular schools compete for smaller slices of the budgetary pie.

And that is what happened in California and the Oakland Unified School District (OUSD). Further complicating the financial situation in the OUSD were years when the district overspent its budget; the district required a state bailout of over $100 million in 2003. Frequent turnover in superintendents (thirteen in twenty years) and the constant churn of school reforms related to the small schools movement, community schools, and charter schools added to the constant budgetary crisis caused by the district's financial mismanagement.[21]

Add in the long-running squabbles between the Board of Education and parents over the district's support of many low-enrollment schools—some as small as 250 students—leading to annual overspending that triggered cuts in the following year's budget. Consider that in 2020–2021, the OUSD had 35,000 students distributed across 81 schools while two other California districts of the same size had 43 and 45 schools. Year after year, the OUSD Board of Education had argued over how many schools to close, often ending up shuttering none or a bare handful after public outcries. Continued funding of so many schools precipitated budgetary crunches, much public bickering, and headlines in Bay Area news media. That was the fiscal situation in the OUSD as the number of charter schools, including community schools, mushroomed.[22]

Charters and regular schools in the OUSD also competed for space. Unused school buildings or ones recently closed, for example, can be used to house charters, a decision the Board of Education made in 2022. But many parents objected to having their neighborhood school closed and then reopened to serve children from other parts of the district attending a new charter school.[23]

Obviously, the entry of charter schools into the OUSD decades ago did not cause the problems the district experienced. Fiscal mismanagement, a swinging-door superintendency, an unceasing flow of new but unconnected reforms, and a deep reluctance to close very small schools are only some of the factors that explain the OUSD's travails in recent decades—not charter schools.

Yet the question of whether the OUSD's charters (including community schools) academically outperformed regular schools remained not only unanswered during the public spats over consolidating small schools and allowing charters to use space in closed buildings but also, at least thus far, unanswerable. As of 2022, I could find no studies of the academic performance of Oakland's charter schools compared to the district's regular schools. State studies of charters, however, have been done.

In California, for example, a 2007 study that compared elementary and secondary charter schools with matched samples of noncharter schools on multiple academic achievement outcomes concluded that

- with student characteristics accounted for, elementary charter schools did not perform as well as elementary noncharters;
- charter middle schools significantly outperformed noncharter middle schools;
- for charter high schools, results are positive but less consistent.[24]

Such mixed results for comparisons in California occur often because of the sample size, study design, and varied quantitative and qualitative methodologies, all of which are commonly of poor quality in educational research and evaluation.[25]

And when it comes to documenting how Oakland teachers teach, I have not found any surveys or reports on how elementary and secondary teachers practice their craft after 2005. Whether the OUSD replicates findings across the country from other charter school teachers who use hybrids of teaching traditions, I cannot say with certainty. Given the evidence of teaching in similar districts that I and other researchers have gathered over the past three decades, my informed guess would be that teacher-centered instruction and its varied hybrids prevailed then.[26]

The entry and growth of charter schools in the OUSD since the early 1990s illustrates well how an innovation adopted amid fiscal mismanagement, shrinking enrollments, and constant turmoil eventually became standard practice as Oakland Unified expanded its charter schools while operating regular neighborhood ones. Expansion occurred through political decisions made by boards of education in the absence of data showing that charters outperformed regular schools in academic achievement or that teaching effectiveness was higher in charter than regular schools. As for teaching practices, limited data suggest that Oakland Unified teachers across both charters and noncharters continued to use teacher-centered instruction with a sprinkling of student-centered pedagogy in some classrooms. As in other urban districts like Oakland, various hybrids of both teaching traditions emerged, with varying degrees of student participation in both elementary and secondary school classrooms. Such a mix of innovative and conserving ways of teaching—of change and stability in the OUSD—capture what has occurred time and again in classrooms, schools, and district organizations in large and small districts across the nation.[27]

Closing Statement

So here again the story of charter schools and the teachers who staff their classrooms is another instance of the double duty that public schools historically performed in American democracy: reform and conserve. As I have shown in answering the six questions about past and present classroom teaching, dynamic conservatism in the US system of schooling, operating since the mid-nineteenth century, continues in 2022.

Why are these questions important to answer? Answers capture then and now the very core of classroom teaching in US public schools. Knowing how teachers have taught in the past, how teaching has remained stable and yet changed over time, and how reformers have made many efforts to improve classroom practices are starting points for grasping the largely unseen complexity, the entangled intricacies, of both schooling and teaching practice.

When that complexity is fully or even partially grasped, reformers committed to improving how teachers teach can make a far better, more accurate road map to follow than ones based on tales from friends or faded memories of sitting in classrooms decades earlier. Hence, each of these questions became a chapter in the book.

In this book, I have blended history with policy to inform policymakers, researchers, practitioners, and parents who seek improvements in their schools and classrooms. Being aware of what past generations of school reformers have designed and put into practice is crucial to the inevitable proposals for changes in schooling and teaching practice that will emerge in years to come.

Of equal importance to school and classroom reformers are the essential skills of parsing the differences between what reformers say, the policies officials adopt, and what teachers actually put into practice after closing the classroom door. Policy talk, policy adoption, and teacher actions in their classrooms are three phases of school reform that too many well-intentioned but ahistorical reformers have ignored.

Again, knowing well the past efforts to alter what happens in schools and classrooms and keeping in mind the dual purposes of tax-supported public schools can reduce the hype and all-too-frequent disappointments that occur in the wake of sputtering or failed reforms.

Achieving public schools' contradictory purposes of reforming and conserving has not been a walk in the park. Constant conflict over public schools' responsibilities has created ongoing dilemmas for school superintendents, principals, and teachers decade after decade. Those dilemmas are as hardwired in US schools as is the double duty of reforming and conserving.

Aspiring reformers need to know in their heads and hearts that these repeated conflicts over what Americans expect of their schools and the incremental changes that have occurred to ease the constant friction account for and explain both stability and change in schooling and classroom practices. Indeed, dynamic conservatism—making changes to preserve stability—has been the hallmark of US schooling and classroom lessons into the twenty-first century. It ain't going away.

Acknowledgments

Writing this book grew from my belief that now was the time to pull together the different strands of my experience as a high school history teacher in the Cleveland and Washington, DC, public schools, as a district administrator in Washington DC, as superintendent in Arlington County, VA, and, finally, as a professor at Stanford University. I have taught over six decades in classrooms where I learned and practiced the complex art of teaching.

During these years, I had also written about the history of teaching in *How Teachers Taught* (1993) and *Hugging the Middle* (2009). And in *Confessions of a School Reformer* (2021), I had delved into my memories of being a student in Pittsburgh public schools, a social studies teacher in Cleveland and Washington, DC, and a professor at Stanford University.

Teaching had been central to my daily work since 1956, but doing research had been important as well. Answering puzzling questions was critical to understanding my encounters in diverse classrooms. And as a professor, for the first time, I had the time not only to teach and observe teachers doing lessons in schools but also to reflect upon my experiences.

As a researcher, then, who had spent years observing teachers in classrooms and plumbing the history of teaching in the United States, I have slowly and, I might add, carefully drawn a few conclusions about how teachers teach. *The Enduring Classroom: Teaching Then and Now* brings together the fruits of my classroom experiences and observations that I have accumulated over a half-century about the practice of teaching.

As any author knows, no book writes itself. Other writers who sought to understand how teachers have taught, both now and in the past, have been helpful. But of equal, if not greater importance, is the support I have received from family and friends. I acknowledge here those who have helped me reach this point in my life when I could write *The Enduring Classroom*.

My two daughters, Sondra and Janice Cuban, and granddaughter, Barbaraciela are foremost in my mind every day. They are my immediate family. My love for them remains unconditional. Decades-long friendships with Nancy Merenstein, Sam Balk, Jane David, Bill Plitt, Sarah Blackstone and Harvey Pressman, Heather Kirkpatrick, Joel Westheimer, David and Soching Brazer, and Milbrey McLaughlin have both stretched and fulfilled me. I am one fortunate but sad old-timer.

Why sad? Although grateful for living a long and full life, I have lost immediate family and dear friends while writing these books. Most of all, I miss my wife, Barbara, who died in 2009. We had fifty-one years together that enriched my life and helped make me and my daughters who we are today. Recent deaths of dear friends David Mazer and Yus Merenstein—separated geographically for decades but nonetheless staying in close touch—hit me hard. Even as I write this acknowledgment, I feel their absence.

After writing nearly two dozen books with various publishers, I returned to the University of Chicago Press. I did so because they had published my first scholarly book—*Urban School Chiefs under Fire* (1976). So, I want to thank Elizabeth Branch Dyson, Executive Editor at the University of Chicago Press, who acquired this book and helpfully prodded me numerous times to sandpaper the manuscript's rough edges.

I acknowledge here also how lucky I have been to have had a career in teaching across varied venues and to have the opportunity to think and write about my experiences in classrooms.

For all of the family and friends who helped me in numerous, often unspoken ways, to write this book, I am grateful. Their help, however, does not relieve me of making clear that any errors or misinterpretations found in this book are mine and mine only.

Notes

Preface

1. Larry Cuban, *How Teachers Taught* (New York: Teachers College Press, 1993), 7.
2. Cuban, *How Teachers Taught*, 7.

Chapter One

1. Wayne Fuller, *The Old Country School* (Chicago: University of Chicago Press, 1982), 203. For firsthand accounts of rural one-room schoolhouse teachers, see Barbara Finkelstein, *Governing the Young: Teacher Behavior in Popular Primary Schools in 19th-Century United States* (Philadelphia: The Falmer Press, 1989).

2. Selma Wassermann is a professor emerita from Simon Fraser University in Vancouver, British Columbia, and a former New York City teacher and reading specialist. She has written widely and extensively from a pedagogically progressive view about reading instruction, science teaching, getting students to think critically, and teacher use of case studies in lessons. The excerpt comes from her book, *This Teaching Life* (Teachers College Press, 2004), 5–6.

3. I have known Gabriel Stewart since he was student in my social studies curriculum and instruction course in the Stanford University teacher education program nearly twenty-five years ago. I had not seen him teach since he was in that program, although we have seen one another on occasion, since we live in the same neighborhood. When I visited Los Altos high school in 2016 to see other teachers, I had stopped into his classroom to say hello. Hearing about my observations, he then invited me into his AP US history class.

Los Altos high school has over 2,200 students (2020), and its demography is mostly minority (in percentages: Latino 27, Asian 27, African American 1, multiracial 8, and white 36). The percentage of students eligible for free and reduced-price lunches (the poverty indicator) is 19 percent. Nine percent of students are learning-disabled, and just over 3 percent of LAHS students are English-language learners.

Academically, 96 percent of the district students graduate high school, and nearly all enter higher education. About 75 percent of students take at least one AP course. LAHS has been rated repeatedly as one of the top high schools (number 60 out of over 1,330 in the state and number 437 in the nation's 26,000 high schools). Nonetheless, there is a gap in achievement between minorities and whites, one that has not shrunk in recent years. The district per-pupil expenditure at the high school is just over $23,000 (2017). See "Mountain View-Los Altos Union High School District," at the Public School Review website: https://www.publicschoolreview.com/california /mountain-view-los-altos-union-high-school-district/626310-school-district.

See also, "Los Altos High School Accountability Report Card, 2019–2020," at: https://www .mvla.net/documents/2020_School_Accountability_Report_Card_-CDE-_Los_Altos_High _School_20210203.pdf.

4. Mark Schug, "Teacher-Centered Instruction: The Rodney Dangerfield of Instruction," in *Where Did Social Studies Go Wrong*," by James Leming et al., a report from the Thomas B. Fordham Foundation, 2003,94; at https://citeseerx.ist.psu.edu/viewdoc/download?doi=10.1.1.46 9.1672&rep=rep1&type=pdf#page=109.

5. Cuban, *How Teachers Taught* (New York: Teachers College Press, 1993), 7.

6. See "The Glossary of Education Reform" at https://www.edglossary.org/direct-instruction/.

7. Wikipedia, "Student-centered Learning" at https://en.wikipedia.org/wiki/Student-centered _learning. Also see, John McCarthy, "Student-Centered Learning: It Starts with the Teacher," on the Edutopia, 2015 website at https://www.edutopia.org/blog/student-centered-learning-starts -with-teacher-john-mccarthy; and Linda Darling-Hammond et al., "Student-Centered Schools," Policy Brief from Stanford Center for Opportunity Policy in Education, June 2014 at https:// edpolicy.stanford.edu/sites/default/files/scope-pub-student-centered-policy.pdf.

8. Montclaire is in the Cupertino School District. The school has just over five hundred students. Of the school enrollment, 46 percent is white, 38 percent Asian, 5 percent are Latino, and the rest are distributed among multiracial, African American, Filipino, and so forth. Those categorized as poor (i.e., eligible for free or discounted lunch) are just over 2 percent of enrollment. According to Auten, many of the parents work for Google and Apple.

The district has a policy of two students per computer. They also provide a tech support person on site. To obtain one iPad for each student, Auten became entrepreneurial. She got twelve from the district and applied for a grant to get a few more. Parents contributed devices, and she corresponded with a University of Michigan professor who acquired the rest through a program he was affiliated with.

9. Teacher accounts of setting up learning centers surged in the early 2000s, but few secondary school teachers had the time or inclination to do the added work of creating, sustaining, and assessing such centers. See Allison Movitz and Kerry Holmes, "Finding Center: How Learning Centers Evolved in a Secondary Student-Centered Classroom," *English Journal* 96, no. 3 (2007): 68–73.

10. In creating this continuum, I reflected on where I would place my teaching over decades. What became obvious to me is that my placement on the continuum depended on when I taught. For example, I began high school teaching in the mid-1950s, and I was wholly teacher-centered, but as the years passed, I slowly incorporated features of student-centered instruction: small-group and independent work, group discussions, student-chosen research projects, and occasional learning centers. So the continuum is time-sensitive to changes in teaching over the course of one's career.

11. Philip Jackson, *Life in Classrooms* (New York: Holt Rinehart and Winston, 1968), 129. This book is a classic beginning point for any researcher, reform-minded policymaker, or parent in understanding the dynamics of classroom teaching and in capturing the nature of a teacher's authority and how it is exerted to achieve both student control and learning. The "Daily Grind" chapter is a solid rendition of teacher-centered instruction and worth the price of the book.

12. Numerous research studies show that one aspect of a teacher-centered approach, called "direct instruction"—explicit and systematic teaching of content and skills—has yielded mar-

ginally higher test scores. See Jean Stockard et al., "The Effectiveness of Direct Instruction Curricula: S Meta-Analysis of a Half-Century of Research," *Review of Educational Research* 88, no. 4 (2018): 487–507. Keep in mind that teacher-centered instruction has come to include features of student-centered teaching in US classrooms since the mid-twentieth century.

13. Joseph Rice, *The Public School System of the United States* (New York: Arno Press, 1969), 130.

14. John Dewey, *The Child and the Curriculum* (Chicago: University of Chicago Press, 1991); John Dewey, *The School and Society* (Chicago: University of Chicago Press, 1991); Lawrence Cremin, *The Transformation of the School* (New York: Vintage, 1961); William Reese, "The Origins of Progressive Education," *History of Education Quarterly* 4, no. 1 (2001): 1–24; for a recent analysis of school field trips, see Jay Greene et al., "The Educational Value of Field Trips," *Education Next* 14, no. 1 (2013), at https://www.educationnext.org/the-educational-value-of-field-trips/.

15. Rice, *Public School System*, 195–97.

16. Kristen Dombkowski, "Will the Real Kindergarten Please Stand Up? Defining and Redefining the Twentieth Century U.S. Kindergarten," *History of Education* 30, no. 6 (2001): 527–45.

17. Barbara Beatty, *Preschool Education in America* (New Haven, CT: Yale University Press, 1995).

18. U.S. Department of Commerce, "1950 Census of Population: School and Kindergarten Enrollment for the United States," 1; online at https://www2.census.gov/library/publications/decennial/1950/pc-14/pc-14-07.pdf.

19. The quotation is from Elizabeth Sherwood, "Building the Kindergarten Curriculum: What Patty Smith Hill and a 1950s Kindergarten Teacher Can Teach Us About Children as Active Learners," *Young Children* 76, no. 4 (2021): 84.

20. I cannot vouch completely for the authenticity of this particular report card. I tried to locate "Margaret Bramer," the school she attended and district, but could not. The report card, however, mirrors many similar ones from the mid-1950s when play, exploration, and learning school habits, listening to the teacher were aims of the kindergarten. The shift to academics, that is, learning to read and calculating numbers to be ready for first grade occurred in subsequent decades. See Lorrie Shepard and Mary Lee Smith, "Escalating Academic Demand in Kindergarten: Counterproductive Policies," *Elementary School Journal* 89, no. 2 (1988): 135–45.

21. Wikipedia, "Matryoshka Doll" at: https://en.wikipedia.org/wiki/Matryoshka_doll.

Chapter Two

1. Thomas Snyder, ed., "120 Years of American Education: A Statistical Portrait," at http://nces.gov/pubs93/93442.pdf; Lisa Borten, "What American Education Was Like 100 Years Ago," at https://stacker.com/stories/3315/what-american-education-was-100-years-ago.

2. Cuban, *How Teachers Taught* (New York: Teachers College Press, 1993), chapters 1 and 6; Richard Elmore, "Structural Reform and Educational Practice, *Educational Researcher* 24, no. 9 (1995): 23–26; Larry Cuban, *Teachers and Machines* (New York: Teachers College Press, 1986).

3. Mary Haywood Metz, "Real School: A Universal Drama amid Disparate Experience," *Journal of Education Policy* 4, no. 5 (1989): 75–91.

4. Jack Schneider, quoted in Valerie Strauss, "Betsy DeVos Insists Public Schools Have Not Changed in More Than a Hundred Years. Why She Is Oh So Wrong," *Washington Post*, October 25, 2019.

5. PBS, "Only a Teacher," at https://www.pbs.org/onlyateacher/timeline.html. Lisa Borten, "What American Education Was Like 100 Years Ago," at https://stacker.com/stories/3315/what-american-education-was-100-years-ago.

6. Alia Wong, "The U.S. Teaching Population Is Getting Bigger, and More Female," *Atlantic*, February 20, 2019 at https://www.theatlantic.com/education/archive/2019/02/the-explosion-of-women-teachers/582622/.

7. Myra Strober and David Tyack, "Why Do Women Teach and Men Manage? A Report on Schools," *Signs* 5, no. 3 (1980): 494–503.

8. Strober and Tyack, "Why Do Women Teach?"

9. Victoria-Maria MacDonald, "Setting the Context: Historical Perspectives on Latino/a Education," in Pedro Pedraza and Melissa Rivera, eds., *Latino Education* (Mahwah, NJ: Lawrence Erlbaum Associates, 2005), 47–73; Ruben Donato and Jarrod Hanson, "Mexican–American Resistance to School Segregation," *Phi Delta Kappan* 100, no. 5 (2019): 39–42.

10. Erica Frankenberg et al., "Harming Our Common Future: Segregated Schools 65 Years after *Brown*," Center for Education and Civil Rights, Penn State University, May 10, 2019.

11. See Benjamin Spock, *The Common Sense Book of Baby and Child Care*, 6th ed. (Mountain View, CA: Ishi Press, 2013).

12. Spock, *Baby and Child Care*; *Common Sense Book*; Paula Fass, "There Used to Be Consensus on How to Raise Kids," *Atlantic*, March 20, 2018 at https://www.theatlantic.com/family/archive/2018/03/america-new-dr-spock/555311/.

13. US Supreme Court decision can be found at http://www.ncbi.nlm.nih.gov/pmc/articles/pmc5766273/.

14. Thomas Snyder, ed., *120 Years of American Education: A Statistical Portrait* (Washington, DC: US Office of Education, National Center for Educational Statistics, 1993), 28.

15. John Wallace et al., "Racial, Ethnic, and Gender Differences among US High School Students, 1991–2005," *Negro Education Review* 59, nos. 1–2 (2008): 47–62; The Civil Rights Project, "Lost Opportunities: How Disparate School Discipline Continues to Drive Differences in the Opportunity to Learn, " October 11, 2020 at https://www.civilrightsproject.ucla.edu/research/k-12-education/school-discipline/lost-opportunities-how-disparate-school-discipline-contin ues-to-drive-differences-in-the-opportunity-to-learn.

16. Wikipedia, "School Corporal Punishment in the United States," at https://en.wikipedia.org/wiki/School_corporal_punishment_in_the_United_States, last edited September 11, 2021; Russel Skiba et al., "Race Is Not Neutral," *School Psychology Review* 40, no. 1 (2011): 85–107.

17. Wikipedia, "Computers in the Classroom," at https://en.wikipedia.org/wiki/Computers_in_the_classroom, last edited September 5, 2021; Audrey Watters, *Teaching Machines: The History of Personalized Learning* (Cambridge, MA: MIT Press, 2021).

18. New Schools Venture Fund and Gallup, "Education Technology Use in Schools" (Washington, DC: Gallup, 2019). The survey sampled 3,210 Pre-K through 12th-grade US public school teachers, 1,163 public school principals, 1,219 district level administrators, and 2,696 public school students from grades 3 through 12; see pp. 4, 9; Benjamin Herold," Schools Handed Out Millions of Digital Devices Under Covid-19: Now Thousands Are Missing," *Education Week*, July 23, 2020.

19. New Schools Venture Fund and Gallup, "Education Technology."

20. Public School Review, "An Overview of the Funding of Public Schools," March 31, 2021, at https://www.publicschoolreview.com/blog/an-overview-of-the-funding-of-public-schools.

21. David McGee, "Report Shows Average Per-Pupil School Spending in VA Schools," *Bristol Herald Courier*, July 20, 2020.

22. US Government Accounting Office, "K-12 Education: Student Population Has Significantly Diversified, but Many Schools Remain Divided Along Racial, Ethnic, and Economic Lines," June 16, 2022, GAO-22–104737; Bruce Fuller et al., "Worsening School Segregation for Latino Children?" *Educational Researcher* 48, no. 7 (2019): 407–20.

23. US Government Accounting Office, "Student Population Has Significantly Diversified, But Many Schools Remain Divided Along Racial, Ethnic, and Economic Lines," GAO-22–104737, June 2022.

24. Alyssa Rafa, Ben Erwin, Bryan Kelley, and Micah Ann Wixom, "50-State Comparison: Charter School Policies," January 28, 2020, Education Commission of the States, at https://www.ecs.org/charter-school-policies/.

Chapter Three

1. Some researchers have spent time in classrooms. John Goodlad, *Behind the Classroom Door* (Worthington, OH: Wadsworth, 1970); Arthur Zilversmit, *Changing Schools: Progressive Education Theory and Practice, 1930–1960* (Chicago: University of Chicago Press, 1993); Larry Cuban, *How Teachers Taught* (New York: Teachers College Press, 1993). See also Joseph Tobin, Yeh Hseuh, and Mayumi Karasawa, *Preschool in Three Cultures Revisited: China, Japan, and the United States* (Chicago: University of Chicago Press, 2011).

2. John Anderer, "Unsung Heroes: 80% of Parents Have New Respect for Teachers Thanks to Coronavirus Quarantine," May 1, 2020, *Study Finds* at https://www.studyfinds.org/unsung-heroes-80-of-parents-have-new-respect-for-teachers-thanks-to-coronavirus-quarantine/; PDK Poll of Public Attitudes Toward the Public Schools, "Frustration in the Schools," September 2019, at https://journals.sagepub.com/doi/abs/10.1177/0031721719871559.

3. Adam Laats, *Fundamentalism and Education in the Scopes Era: God, Darwin, and the Roots of America's Culture Wars* (New York: Palgrave MacMillan, 2010); Wikipedia, "School Prayer in the United States," last edited September 19, 2021 at https://en.wikipedia.org/wiki/School_prayer_in_the_United_States; Steven Sawchuk, "What Is Critical Race Theory and Why Is It under Attack?" *Education Week*, May 18, 2021. On the masking controversy, see Anna Kamenetz, "After 2 Years, Growing Calls to Take Masks Off Children in School," January 28, 2022, *NPR-KQED*, at https://www.npr.org/2022/01/28/1075842341/growing-calls-to-take-masks-off-children-in-school.

4. I am indebted to the work of sociologist Dan Lortie in his classic work, *Schoolteacher* (Chicago: University of Chicago Press, 1975). Nearly a half-century ago, Lortie, using 94 interviews with secondary and elementary school teachers in the Boston metropolitan area and a survey of 6,500 teachers in Dade County, FLA, captured the nature of teaching, the sentiments of teachers, and the overall structures and processes that shaped the work of classroom teachers. For anyone investigating the influence of structures on teaching and the sentiments teachers have about children and learning, reading *Schoolteacher* is a beginning point.

As noted in chapter 1, Philip Jackson's *Life in the Classroom* (New York: Holt Rinehart and Winston, 1968) is also a must read for anyone who wishes to understand the nature of teaching in elementary schools. Both Lortie and Jackson have contributed a great deal to my understanding of my experience of fourteen years teaching in Cleveland and Washington, DC, and the many observations I have made of classrooms as a superintendent and researcher.

5. Philip Selznick, "Institutionalism 'Old' and 'New,'" *Administrative Science Quarterly* 41, no. 2 (1996): 270–77; also see Johannes Lindner, "Institutional Stability and Change: Two Sides of the Same Coin," *Journal of European Public Policy* 10, no. 6 (2003): 912–35.

6. 53rd Annual PDK Poll of the Public's Attitudes Toward the Public Schools, press release, 9/2/21.

7. Lisa Suhay, "Transgender Bathroom Battles: How Some Parents See It," *Christian Science Monitor*, May 21, 2016; Jonathan Zimmerman, "Why the Culture Wars in Schools Are Worse Than Ever Before," *Politico Magazine*, September 19, 2021 at https://www.politico.com/news /magazine/2021/09/19/history-culture-wars-schools-america-divided-512614.

8. NCES, "Public School Enrollment Dropped 3 Percent in 2020–2021," June 28, 2021 at: https://nces.ed.gov/whatsnew/press_releases/06_28_2021.asp. On public confidence in schools, see Megan Brenan, "Gallup News," August 12, 2020.

9. Desiree Carver-Thomas and Linda Darling-Hammond, *Teacher Turnover: Why It Matters and What We Can Do About It* (Palo Alto, CA: Learning Policy Institute, 2017).

10. I do not include Teach for America and other alternative certification programs in my analysis because they produce a tiny fraction of new teachers entering urban classrooms, where most novices are placed. While many TFA teachers stay beyond their two-year commitment, the vast majority are leavers. See Wikipedia, "Teach for America" at https://en.wikipedia.org/wiki /Teach_For_America, last edited October 12, 2021.

11. Congressional Research Service, "Teacher Preparation Policies and Issues in the Higher Education Act," November 16, 2018, 3. For the past decade, enrollment in teacher preparation programs across the country have declined. The Covid-19 pandemic accelerated that trend. See Madeline Will, "Fewer People Are Getting Teacher Degrees: Prep Programs Sound the Alarm," *Education Week*, March 22, 2022; https://www.edweek.org/teaching-learning/fewer-peo ple-are-getting-teacher-degrees-prep-programs-sound-the-alarm/2022/03.

12. Geraldine Clifford and James Guthrie, *Ed School* (Chicago: University of Chicago Press, 1988); David Labaree, *The Trouble with Ed Schools* (New Haven, CT: Yale University Press, 2004); Marilyn Cochran-Smith et al., "Critiquing Teacher Preparation Research: An Overview of the Field, Part II, *Journal of Teacher Education* 66, no. 2 (2015): 109–21. For a more critical look at the field, see Arthur Levine, *Educating School Teachers* (Washington, DC: The Education Schools Project, 2006), 5.

A personal note. I graduated as a certified teacher from the University of Pittsburgh in 1955. The country was in the midst of an economic recession and getting a position was difficult. After being turned down repeatedly, I got a job teaching high school biology (my minor) in McKees-port, PA, outside of Pittsburgh. I was paid $2,000 for the year. I then found a social studies job in a Cleveland high school in 1956 and taught there for seven years before moving to Washington, DC, to teach at Cardozo High School in 1963.

13. Jurgen Herbst, "Nineteenth Century Normal Schools in the United States: A Fresh Look," *History of Education* 9, no. 3 (1980): 219–37.

14. Etta Hollins and Connor Warner, "Evaluating the Clinical Component of Teacher Preparation Programs (National Academy of Education Committee on Evaluating and Improving Teacher Preparation Programs, 2021). Ken Zeichner, a teacher educator at the University of Wisconsin (Madison) for over three decades and later at the University of Washington details his journey from elementary school teaching to tenured professor. He lays out nicely the problems and dilemmas facing teacher educators in the courses they teach, connections to regular school teachers who work with student-teachers from the university, and the clinical experience university students have in schools. See "Becoming a Teacher Educator: A Personal Perspective," *Teaching and Teacher Education* 21 (2005): 117–24.

15. For examples of common criticisms, see Jennifer Medina, "Teacher Training Termed Mediocre," *New York Times*, October 22, 2009. Alternative routes into classrooms apart from university courses and practice teaching have increased since the 1980s (e.g., Teach for America). Nearly all states provide options for adults to become certified teachers apart from enrolling in university-sponsored courses, such as Relay University's program training. See Brendan Lowe, "A Decade After It Promised to Reinvent Teacher Prep, Relay Is Producing a Much-Needed, More Diverse Teaching Corps," *The 74*, October 6, 2019.

Nearly all new teachers (95 percent) are licensed to teach through university-approved programs. See Gene Glass, "Alternative Certification of Teachers" (Education Policy Research Unit, 2008) at http://epicpolicy.org/publication/alternative-certification-of-teachers.

16. David Labaree, *The Trouble with Ed Schools* (New Haven, CT: Yale University Press, 2004), chapters 3 and 7.

17. The classic example is what university educators often called "classroom management" and public school teachers referred to as "discipline" or "controlling students" in order for them to learn. Over time, university educators incorporated into their teacher education curriculum either courses or short modules where "classroom management" techniques were taught. See, for example, Gordon Eisenman et al., "Bringing Reality to Classroom Management in Teacher education," *Professional Educator* (2015), at https://files.eric.ed.gov/fulltext/EJ1062280.pdf.

18. Cindy Bourdo, "The Biggest Lesson of My First Year Teaching," *Edutopia*, February 11, 2019. For examples of books written by first-year teachers, see Esme' Codell, *Educating Esme'* (Chapel Hill, NC: Algonquin Books of Chapel Hill, 2009); Pearl Rock Kane, ed., *My First Year As a Teacher* (New York: Penguin Group, 1996).

19. Lucinda Gray et al., "Public School Teacher Attrition and Mobility in the First Five Years" (National Center for Education Statistics, April 2015); National Center for Teacher Residencies, "Equitable Access to Teachers of Color Matters," at https://nctresidencies.org/.

Residency programs where aspiring teachers spend a year with an experienced teacher in an on-site apprenticeship while attending after-school university classes have helped new teachers to adjust to the unrelenting demands of classroom teaching. Many of these programs recruit and train minority teachers so that after a year they have become licensed and earned a Master's degree. See https://nctresidencies.org/

20. Susan Kardos et al., "Counting on Colleagues: New Teachers Encounter the Professional Cultures of Their Schools," *Educational Administration Quarterly* 37, no. 2 (2001): 250–90.

21. Richard Scott and John Meyer, *Organizational Environments: Ritual and Rationality* (Newbury Park, CA: Sage, 1992).

22. Carl Kaestle, *Pillars of the Republic: Common Schools and American Society, 1780–1860* (New York: Hill and Wang, 1983); Adam Laats, "Joseph Lancaster and the Roots of America's Public Schools, 1800–1840," at https://adamlaats.net/2018/05/09/toe-the-line-joseph-lancaster-and-the-delusion-of-early-school-reform/.

23. William Reese, *Testing Wars in the Public Schools: A Forgotten History* (Cambridge, MA: Harvard University Press, 2013); Wikipedia, "Community Colleges in the United States," at https://en.wikipedia.org/wiki/Community_colleges_in_the_United_States, last edited October 31, 2021.

24. David K. Cohen and Jal D. Mehta, "Why Reform Sometimes Succeeds: Understanding the Conditions That Produce Reforms That Last," *American Educational Research Journal* 54, no. 4 (2017): 644–90.

25. Ran Abramitzky and Leah Bouston, "Immigration in American Economic History," *Journal of Economic Literature* 55, no. 4 (2017): 1311–45. For graduation rate (2019), see Emma Kerr, "See High School Graduation Rates by State," *US News & World Report*, April 28, 2019, at https://www.usnews.com/education/best-high-schools/articles/see-high-school-graduation-rates-by-state.

26. Max Roser and Esteban Ortiz-Ospina, "Primary and Secondary Education," in *Our World in Data*, at https://ourworldindata.org/primary-and-secondary-education; Organization for Economic and Community Development (OECD), "Education in China: A Snapshot," at https://www.oecd.org/china/Education-in-China-a-snapshot.pdf.

27. Early progressive educator Colonel Francis Wayland Parker founded the Chicago private school that later carried his name in 1901. See https://www.fwparker.org/; Caroline Pratt established the City and Country School located in New York City's Greenwich Village in 1914. See https://en.wikipedia.org/wiki/City_and_Country_School. Founded in 1929, The School in Rose Valley, like the others, is an elementary school outside Philadelphia. See https://www.theschoolinrosevalley.org/about-srv/.

28. David Labaree has analyzed how public and private goods compete in American views of the public school. See "Public Goods, Private Goods: The American Struggle Over Educational Goals," *American Educational Research Journal* 34, no. 1 (1997): 39–81.

29. David Tyack and William Tobin, "The 'Grammar" of Schooling': Why Has It Been So Hard to Change?" *American Educational Research Journal* 31, no. 3 (1994): 453–79. For a concise definition of the Carnegie Unit, see Carnegie Foundation for the Advancement of Teaching, "What Is the Carnegie Unit," at https://www.carnegiefoundation.org/faqs/ -unit/.

30. Charter Schools in Perspective, "Key Facts about Charter Schools," updated 2018, at http://www.in-perspective.org/pages/introduction.

31. Middletown City School District, "Central Academy," at https://www.middletowncityschools.com/central-academy/about-us-16/about-us-16/.

32. Grant Wiggins, "A True Test: Toward More Authentic and Equitable Assessment," *Phi Delta Kappan*, May 1989, 703–13.

33. Short articles on Deborah Meier and Ted Sizer can be found as Wikipedia entries under each one's name.

34. Young Whan Choi, "Oakland's Graduate Capstone Project: It's About Equity," Learning Policy Institute Blog, October 26, 2017.

35. A few of these reforms aimed at altering how schools operate in these years follow: competency-based instruction (see https://en.wikipedia.org/wiki/Competency-based_learning); multi-age groupings (see https://en.wikipedia.org/wiki/Multi-age_classroom); "personalized learning" (see https://en.wikipedia.org/wiki/Personalized_learning). Keep in mind, however, that much variation in each of these reforms is common when they are implemented in particular schools and districts. Context remains crucial when putting an innovation into practice.

36. Matt Zalaznick, "Mask Tracker: Mandates Are Expiring in All States But One," *DA District Administration*, March 10, 2022

37. AIR National Survey of Public Education's Response to Covid-19, Joanne Carminucci, et al., "Student Attendance and Enrollment Loss in 2020–2021," June 2021, at https://www.air.org/sites/default/files/2021–07/research-brief-covid-survey-student-attendance-june-2021_0.pdf.

38. *New York Times*, "Coronavirus in the United States: Latest Map and Case Count," updated March 10, 2022, at https://www.nytimes.com/interactive/2021/us/covid-cases.html.

39. I do not include school closures that resulted from policy decisions, such as the closing of

Prince Edward County schools in Virginia in 1959 to avoid desegregating their schools. See https://www.virginiahistory.org/collections-and-resources/virginia-history-explorer/civil-rights -movement-virginia/closing-prince. For Seattle schools, see "American Influenza Epidemic: Seattle Washington," University of Michigan Center for the History of Medicine, at https://www.influenzaarchive.org/cities/city-seattle.html#; for Philadelphia, see Alfred Crosby, *Americas Forgotten Pandemic: The Influenza of 1918* (New York: Cambridge University Press, 2003), 74, 85.

40. Lawrence A. Cremin, *The Transformation of the School: Progressivism in American Education, 1876–1957* (New York: Vintage Books, 1964); Herbert M. Kliebard, *The Struggle for the American Curriculum, 1893–1958* (Boston: Routledge and Kegan Paul, 1986); and Diane Ravitch, *Left Back: A Century of Failed School Reforms* (New York: Simon & Schuster, 2000); Tracy Steffes, *School, Society, and State: A New Education to Govern Modern America, 1890–1940* (Chicago: University of Chicago Press, 2012); David Gamson, *The Importance of Being Urban: Designing the Progressive School District, 1890–1940* (Chicago: University of Chicago Press, 2019).

41. Michael Hines, "In Chicago, Schools Closed during a 1937 Polio Epidemic and Kids Learned from Home—Over the Radio," *Washington Post*, April 3, 2020.

42. Douglas Harris, *Charter School City* (Chicago: University of Chicago Press, 2020).

43. Rebecca Klein, "These Are the Schools That Hurricane Katrina Destroyed," *HuffPost*, August 26, 2015; Kate Babineau et al, "The State of Public Education in New Orleans, 2019–2020," The Cowen Institute at Tulane University, at https://files.eric.ed.gov/fulltext/ED607281.pdf.

44. Jal Mehta, "Make Schools More Human," *New York Times*, December 23, 2020.

45. Valerie Strauss, "Big Questions about 2021 Standardized Test Scores," *Washington Post*, September 23, 2021.

46. Sydney Johnson, "Hundreds of Thousands of California Students Won't Take Standardized Tests This Spring," *EdSource*, May 4, 2021; Mark Lieberman, "Five Things You Need to Know about Student Absences During Covid-19," *Education Week*, October 16, 2020.

47. Erin Richards et al., "A year into the pandemic, thousands of students still can't get reliable WiFi for school. The digital divide remains worse than ever," *USA TODAY*, February 4, 2021.

48. David Berliner and Gene Glass, "Why Bother Testing in 2021?" *Diane Ravitch's Blog*, August, 31, 2020, at https://nepc.colorado.edu/blog/why-bother.

49. Julia Kaufman et al., *U.S. Teachers' Support of Their State Standards and Assessments* (Santa Monica, CA: RAND Corporation, 2017).

50. Valerie Strauss, "It Looks Like the Beginning of the End of America's Obsession with Student Standardized Tests," *Washington Post*, June 21, 2020.

51. Arrman Kyaw, "Majority of Americans Want Standardized Testing Requirements Removed," Diverse Issues in Higher Education, February 1, 2021, at www.diverseeducation.com /news-roundup/article/15108581/majority-of-americans-want-standardized-testing-require ments-removed.

Chapter Four

1. Joseph Rice, *The Public School System of the United States* (New York: Arno Press and the New York Times, 1969), 241–42.

2. The teacher in this Indianapolis school over a century ago had established one place in the classroom that teachers in the 1970s might call a "learning center." I take up this change in teaching practice later in this chapter.

3. Ronald Kellum, "The Influence of Francis Wayland Parker's Pedagogy on the Pedagogy of John Dewey," *Journal of Thought* 18, no. 1 (1983): 77–91; Wikipedia, "Maria Montessori," at https://en.wikipedia.org/wiki/Maria_Montessori; see also "Ella Flagg Young: American Educator," at https://www.britannica.com/biography/Ella-Flagg-Young.

4. This distinction between "administrative" and "pedagogical" progressives comes from David Tyack, *The One Best System* (Cambridge, MA: Harvard University Press, 1974), 128. Also see David Tyack and Elisabeth Hansot, *Managers of Virtue* (New York: Basic Books, 1982), 105–14. For an earlier study of "scientific management" and the appeal for educators of the efficiency movement at the beginning of the twentieth century, see Raymond Callahan, *Education and the Cult of Efficiency* (Chicago: University of Chicago Press, 1962).

5. Tina Trujillo, "The Modern Cult of Efficiency: Intermediary Organizations and the New Scientific Management," *Educational Policy* 28, no. 2 (2014): 207–32.

6. See Lawrence Cremin, *The Transformation of the School: Progressivism in American Education, 1876–1957* (New York: Vintage, 1962); Herbert Kliebard, *The Struggle for the American Curriculum, 1893–1958* (London: Routledge, 2004); Diane Ravitch, *Left Back: A Century of Failed School Reforms* (New York: Simon and Schuster, 2000).

7. The theorists and practitioners named in this paragraph can all be found in Wikipedia entries. Of course, these progressives were hardly monolithic; they had sharply different views simply because each had a different definition of what was "progressive" in schooling and classroom practice. The larger point is that there is continuity between generations of progressives, even though they held different views. Historian David Labaree concluded what both generations of reformers had in common: "Child-centered progressivism is still standing outside the walls of the school trying to break in, so it continues to define itself in opposition to the way things are in schools, and it continues to call on Dewey's name for support." See "How Dewey Lost," November 2, 2019, at https://davidlabaree.com/2019/09/02/how-dewey-lost/.

8. Pat Graham, *Progressive Education: From Arcady to Academe* (New York: Teachers College Press, 1967).

9. I entered the phrase "progressive education" in the Ngram Viewer on December 2, 2021, at https://books.google.com/ngrams/graph?content=Progressive+education&year_start=1800 &year_end=2019&corpus=26&smoothing=3&direct_url=t1%3B%2CProgressive%20education %3B%2Cc0#t1%3B%2CProgressive%20education%3B%2Cc0.

10. One listing of both public and private schools that I used is the Progressive Education Network at https://progressiveeducationnetwork.org/partners/. My own contacts with schools over the past quarter-century have included progressive schools.

11. Steve Farkas, Jean Johnson, et al., "Different Drummers: How Teachers of Teachers View Public Education," (Brooklyn, NY: Public Agenda Foundation, 1997), 10; David Labaree, *The Trouble with Ed Schools* (New Haven, CT: Yale University Press, 2004); see chapter 7.

12. The PEN journal can be found at https://issuu.com/progressiveeducationnetwork0/docs /2021.03_pen_5/7.

13. The website for *Edutopia* contains its history as an organization, mission, strategies to achieve that mission, and other information about both the magazine and the progressive community of educators that it serves. See https://www.edutopia.org/.

14. *A Nation at Risk: The Imperative for Educational Reform* (Washington, DC: National Commission on Excellence in Education: Superintendent of Documents, US Government Printing Office, 1983); Sarah Garland, "Why Is a Reagan-Era Report Driving Today's Education Reform," *The Hechinger Report*, August 17, 2014.

15. Brian Rowan et al., "School Improvement By Design: Lessons from a Study of Comprehensive School Reform Programs" (Philadelphia: Consortium for Policy Research in Education, 2009) at https://repository.upenn.edu/cgi/viewcontent.cgi?article=1025&context=cpre_researchreport.

16. Rowan et al., "School Improvement By Design," n.p.

17. Robert Slavin et al., "Research In, Research Out: The Role of Research in the Development and Scale-Up of Success for All," June 2005 at https://www.successforall.org/wp-content/uploads/2016/02/research-in-research-out-06-10-05.pdf. See also Alan Cheung et al., "Success for All: A Quantitative Synthesis of U.S. Evaluations," *Journal of Research on Educational Effectiveness* 14, no. 1 (2021): 90–115.

18. Richard Correnti and Brian Rowan, "Opening Up the Black Box: Literacy Instruction in Three Comprehensive School Reform Programs," *American Educational Research Journal*, 2007, 44(2), 298–338. The quote is on 305–306.

19. Zachary Jason, "The Battle over Charter Schools," *Harvard Ed. Magazine*, Summer 2017, at https://www.gse.harvard.edu/news/ed/17/05/battle-over-charter-schools.

20. National Center for Education Statistics, "Fast Facts: Charter Schools," at https://nces.ed.gov/fastfacts/display.asp?id=30.

21. Jay Mathews, " 'No Excuses Schools' Make No Excuse for Updating Their Approach," *Washington Post*, August 2, 2019.

22. Thomas Dee and Brian Jacob, "The Impact of No Child Left Behind upon Students, Teachers, and Schools," *Brookings Papers on Economic Activity*, November 2009: 149–207; Joseph Pedulla et al, "Perceived Effects of State-Mandated Testing Programs on Teaching and Learning: Findings from a National Survey of Teachers" (Boston College's Lynch School Faculty Publications, 2003).

23. Susan Semel and Alan Sadovnik, "The Contemporary Small-School Movement: Lessons from the History of Progressive Education," *Teachers College Record* 110, no. 9 (2008): 1744–71. Also see Nel Noddings, "What Does It Mean to Educate the Whole Child," *Educational Leadership* 63 (2005): 8–13.

24. Ibid. Semel and Alan Sadovnik, "Contemporary Small-School Movement." Also see Wikipedia, "Small Schools Movement," at https://en.wikipedia.org/wiki/Small_schools_movement. For what occurred in the Oakland Unified School District, see Milbrey McLaughlin et al., *The Way We Do School: The Making of Oakland's Full-Service Community School District* (Cambridge, MA: Harvard Education Press, 2020).

25. Richard Day and JoAnn Ewalt, "Education Reform in Kentucky: Just What the Court Ordered," *Encompass*, Eastern Kentucky University, 2013, at https://encompass.eku.edu/cgi/viewcontent.cgi?article=1469&context=fs_research. For a description of the Prichard Committee of the General Assembly, see https://prichardcommittee.org/history/.

26. Patricia Kannapel et al., "Implementation of Kentucky Nongraded Primary Program," 2000, *Education Policy Analysis Archives*, Arizona State University, Tempe, Arizona.

27. Rosann Tung, *Including Performance Assessment in Accountability Systems* (Boston, MA: Center for Collaborative Education, 2012), 15–17.

28. Kannapel et al., "Kentucky Nongraded Primary Program."

29. Kannapel et al., "Kentucky Nongraded Primary Program."

30. For example, the charter school law in Washington, DC, led to one of the first nongraded primaries in the District of Columbia. Four teachers created one at Truesdell Elementary School. See Ruth Yodaiken, "Non-Graded School Brings Innovation, Optimism," *Washington Post*, September 15, 1994; and National School Choice Week Team, "Kentucky School

Choice Roadmap," November 12, 2021, at https://schoolchoiceweek.com/guide-school-choice
-kentucky/.

31. Wikipedia, "Learning Centers in American Elementary Schools," at https://en.wikipedia
.org/wiki/Learning_centers_in_American_elementary_schools.

32. I have no documents or archives to draw from to reconstruct what I did in these learning
centers. I rely only on memory and a few entries that I made in my personal journal.

33. John Steele Gordon, "John Rockefeller Sr." Philanthropy Roundtable, at https://www
.philanthropyroundtable.org/resource/john-rockefeller-sr/.

34. Wikipedia, "John D. Rockefeller," at https://en.wikipedia.org/wiki/John_D._Rockefeller.
See also Richard Hofstadter, "Antitrust in America," *Commentary* 38, no. 2 (1964): 47–53.

35. Some readers may question my use of only two examples of lessons I observed and
my own experience a half-century ago to make the point that hybrids of teacher-centered and
student-centered instruction exist after a century of progressive reformers' efforts to transform
teaching from wholly teacher-centered to wholly student-centered. Finding out how teachers
teach then and now has been most difficult (I explain why in chapter 5), given the lack of direct observations of lessons and reliance upon teachers' self-reports. I use these examples as
placeholders until other researchers can establish better than I have how teachers taught then
and now.

Chapter Five

1. Layal Liverpool, "Coronavirus: WHO Announces Greek Alphabet Naming Scheme for
Variants," *New Scientist*, June 1, 2021, at https://www.newscientist.com/article/2279063-corona
virus-who-announces-greek-alphabet-naming-scheme-for-variants/.

2. Eliza Kinsey et al., "School Closures during Covid-19: Opportunities for Innovation in
Meal Service," *American Journal of Public Health*, October 7, 2020, at https://ajph.aphapublica
tions.org/doi/10.2105/AJPH.2020.305875; Benjamin Herold, "Schools Handed Out Millions of
Digital Devices under Covid-19: Now, Thousands are Missing," *Education Week*, July 23, 2020.

3. I chose these years because in an earlier book, *Hugging the Middle* (New York: Teachers
College Press, 2009), I had updated teaching practices between the 1990s and 2005 (My earlier
book, *How Teachers Taught* described teaching through the early 1990s).

4. Julia Kaufman and Melissa Diliberti, "Teachers Are Not All Right," Evidence Project at
CPRE, January 2021.

5. Laura Desimone, et al., "Survey Measures of Classroom Instruction: Comparing Student
and Teacher Reports," *Educational Policy* 24, no. 2 (2009): 267–329. There have been surveys
where students evaluate the performance of their teachers. Since they judge teachers' perfor-
mances rather than describe what occurs during lessons, I have not included such surveys.

6. Carly Berwick, "During Coronavirus, a Teacher Describes the Scramble to Go Digital,"
Edutopia, March 12, 2020.

7. Clare Halloran, et al., "Pandemic School Mode and Student Test Scores: Evidence from
U.S. States," National Bureau of Economic Research, November 2021, Working Paper 29497.

8. Halloran, et al., "Pandemic School Mode."

9. Gaea Leinhardt, et al., "Introduction and Integration of Classroom Routines by Expert
Teachers," *Curriculum Inquiry* 17, no. 2 (1987): 135–76.

10. Margaret Eisenhart, et al., "Teacher Beliefs: Definitions, Findings, and Directions." *Educational Policy* 2, no. 1 (1988): 51–70.

11. See, for example, Brian Rowan and Richard Correnti, "Studying Reading Instruction with Teacher Logs: Lessons from the Study of Instructional Improvement," *Educational Researcher*, 2009, 38(2), 120–131.

12. Laura Cutler and Steve Graham, "Primary Grade Writing Instruction: A National Survey," *Journal of Educational Psychology* 100, no. 4 (2008): 908.

13. Cutler and Graham, "Primary Grade Writing," 915.

14. Cutler and Graham, "Primary Grade Writing," 912.

15. Cutler and Graham, "Primary Grade Writing," 912.

16. Cutler and Graham, "Primary Grade Writing," 918.

17. Patricia Lauer, et al., "The Influence of Standards on K-12 Teaching and Student Learning: A Research Synthesis," August 2005, Mid-Continent Regional Laboratory. For this summary, I focus only on the math curriculum standards.

18. Lauer, et al., "Influence of Standards," 39–40.

19. Brian Rowan and Richard Correnti, "Studying Reading Instruction with Teacher Logs: Lessons from the Study of Instructional Improvement," *Educational Researcher* 38, no. 2 (2009): 120–31.

20. David Cohen and Jal Mehta, "Why Reform Sometimes Succeeds: Understanding the Conditions That Produce Reforms That Last," *American Educational Journal of Research* 54, no. 4 (2017): 644–90.

21. D'Lanie Pelletier, "First-Year Educator on Lessons Learned While Teaching Amid CO-VID," University of Connecticut, Neag School of Education, July 9, 2021.

22. Joe Heim, "Pandemic Teaching, in Their Words," *Washington Post*, October 6, 2020.

23. Jessica Winter, "Who Gets the Blame When Schools Shut Down," *New Yorker*, "Daily Comment," January 7, 2022.

24. As I write in March 2022, statistics on fully vaccinated teachers and students across the nation vary tremendously. While California has mandated that all school staff be fully vaccinated, other states have not. Some states diluted the requirement; in others, it remains unenforced. Matt Barnum, "Delayed, Diluted, or Non Nonexistent: Vaccine Mandates for School Staff Stall Out," *Chalkbeat*, November 3, 2021; *New York Times*, "See How Vaccinations Are Going in Your County and State," February 18, 2022, at https://www.nytimes.com/interactive/2020/us /covid-19-vaccine-doses.html; Mike Antonucci, "Are 90 Percent of Teachers Really Vaccinated Against Covid-19? The Numbers Say Otherwise," *The 74*, August 10, 2021, at https://www.the 74million.org/article/analysis-are-90-percent-of-teachers-really-vaccinated-against-covid -19-the-numbers-say-otherwise/.

25. Donna St. George, et al., "How the Pandemic Is Reshaping Education," *Washington Post*, March 15, 2021; Frederick Hess, "Education After the Pandemic," American Enterprise Institute, January 3, 2022, at https://www.aei.org/articles/education-after-the-pandemic/.

26. Yong Zhao, "COVID-19 as a Catalyst for Educational Change," *Prospects* 49 (2020): 29–33; Jal Mehta, "Make Schools More Human," *New York Times*, December 23, 2020.

Chapter Six

1. Ruben Donato and Jarrod Hanson, "Mexican-American Resistance to School Segregation," *Phi Delta Kappan*, January 21, 2019; Roberto Rodriguez, "The Origins and History of the Chicano Movement." Occasional Paper #7 (The Julian Samora Research Institute, Michigan State University, East Lansing, Michigan, 1996); Mario Garcia and Ellen McCracken, eds., "Rewriting

the Chicano Movement: New Histories of Mexican American Activism in the Civil Rights Era" (Tucson: University of Arizona Press, 2021); Nadra Nittle, "History of the Chicano Movement," *ThoughtCo*, February 16, 2021, at thoughtco.com/chicano-movement-brown-and-proud-2834583.

2. Taylor Branch, *Parting the Waters* (New York: Simon and Schuster, 2007).

3. Louis Sahagun, "East L. A., 1968: 'Walkout!' The day high school students helped ignite the Chicano power movement," *Los Angeles Times*, March 1, 2028.

4. Sahagun, "East L.A., 1968."

5. Mario T. García, and Sal Castro. *Blowout! : Sal Castro and the Chicano Struggle for Educational Justice* (Chapel Hill: The University of North Carolina Press, 2011), 2 . Also, a HBO film called *Walkout* came out in 2006 that focused more on activist students at Garfield and in Castro's class. See: https://en.wikipedia.org/wiki/Walkout_(film)

6. Because of his part in the walkouts, Castro was arrested and eventually released along with other activists. The LAUSD later transferred Castro to a series of other high schools before he left the district. See Wikipedia, "Sal Castro," at https://en.wikipedia.org/wiki/Sal_Castro; Elaine Woo, "Sal Castro Dies at 79: L. A. teacher played role in 1968 protests," *Los Angeles Times*, April 15, 2013.

7. Wikipedia, "Sal Castro," at https://en.wikipedia.org/wiki/Sal_Castro.

8. Jamison White and Matt Hieronimus, "How Many Charter Schools and Students Are There?" National Alliance for Public Charter Schools, February 9, 2022; Arianna Prothero, "At 25th Anniversary Mark, Author of First Charter School Law Reflects on Movement," *Education Week*, June 3, 2016.

9. Between 2011 and 2013, I served on the Board of Trustees of Leadership Public Schools. The four high schools we oversaw were charters in the San Francisco Bay area.

10. Some charter schools do have unions and negotiated contracts with charter boards. See Ashley Jochim and Lesley Lavery, "An Unlikely Bargain: Why Charter School Teachers Unionize and What Happens When They Do," Center for Reinventing Public Education, March 2019, at https://files.eric.ed.gov/fulltext/ED594061.pdf.

11. White and Hieronimus, "How Many Charter Schools?" tables 3.3 and 3.4.

12. White and Hieronimus, "How Many Charter Schools?" table 3.5.

13. Matt Barnum, "Where Do the Nation's Big Charter Boosters Send Their Cash? More and More to Charter Networks," *Chalkbeat*, November 13, 2017.

14. Gary Miron, "Descriptions and Brief History of Charter Schools," in *The Wiley Handbook of School Choice*, ed. Nina Buchanan and Robert Fox (New York: John Wiley, 2017), 224–51.

15. Christopher Lubienski, "Innovation in Education Markets: Theory and Evidence on the Impact of Competition and Choice in Charter Schools," *American Educational Research Journal* 40, no. 2 (2003): 395–443.

16. For KIPP, see Jay Mathews, *Work Hard, Be Nice* (New York: Algonquin Books, 2009). For Aspire, see Susan Colby and Kimberly Wicoff, "Aspire Public Schools: From 10 Schools to Six Million Kids," The Bridgespan Group, February 2006, at https://eric.ed.gov/?id=ED504144.

17. In the half-century that I have observed teachers teach in public elementary and secondary schools, I have developed these criteria for judging a lesson. I know that other teacher supervisors and academic specialists would have different standards and benchmarks but in the interest of transparency, these are the criteria I used. Note that one criterion is absent: what did students learn? As an observer, more often than not, I could not determine what and how much students learned during the lesson. Had I observed a sequence of lessons and seen students'

written and oral work, I might have been able to judge student learning. That was not the case for the observations I include in this chapter.

18. Observing and judging single lessons across two different academic subjects is dicey simply because these are two different disciplines, each with its own content and methodological imperatives. Also the sample of one lesson may be unreliable in the full sweep of lessons each teacher teaches weekly, monthly, and the entire school year. Moreover, observers differ in the criteria they use in observing lessons. These considerations might well raise questions in readers' minds about what I conclude. Readers will have to judge the fairness of my conclusions.

19. Ellen Goldring and Xiu Cravens, "Teachers Academic Focus on Learning in Charter and Non-Charter Schools," Paper prepared for the National Conference on Charter School Research at Vanderbilt University, September 28, 2006, 27.

20. For KIPP schools and student numbers, see website: https://www.kipp.org/kipp -foundation/.

21. Jill Tucker, "Bailed-Out Oakland Schools Are Back in Financial Trouble," *San Francisco Chronicle*, January 3, 2017; "A New OUSD School Board, Same Old Budget Challenges," GO Public Schools Oakland, 2020, at https://gopublicschoolsoakland.org/wp-content/uploads/2020 /10/GO-Policy-Brief-A-New-OUSD-School-Board-Same-Old-Budget-Challenges.pdf.

22. Matthew Green, "Why Does Oakland Have So Many Small Schools?" *KQED*, February 15, 2019; Ali Tadayon, "Oakland Students, Teachers, Community to Fight 11 School Closures, Mergers, Reductions," *Ed Source*, February 9, 2022.

23. Ashley McBride, "OUSD Will Lease More Space to Charters, amid School-Closure Turmoil," *The Oaklandside*, March 24, 2022.

24. Eric Crane, et al., "California Charter Schools: Measuring Their Performance," *EdSource* report, June 2007, 8–12.

25. Angela Velez, "Evaluating Research Methods: Assumptions, Strengths, and Weaknesses of Three Educational Research Paradigms," *Academic Exchange Extra* (2008).

26. I note the absence of recent studies of how Oakland teachers teach in their charter, community and regular schools. I looked at patterns of teaching in Oakland schools between 1993 and 2005 by examining photos in high school yearbooks and looking at archival sources in schools. In observing teachers who volunteered to let me observe their lessons, I also took photos of both secondary and elementary school classrooms in 2005. In the data I collected for Oakland schools, covering more than a decade, forty-nine elementary school teachers reported they used whole-group instruction 72 percent of the time for most or part of the lessons they taught. Over half of these teachers also combined small-group and independent work in a lesson.

In Oakland secondary schools, from which I had 161 reports, 63 percent of the teachers reported that they used whole-group instruction for all or part of their lessons. The photos and observations also showed that 34 percent of Oakland teachers reported often that they used small groups and independent work during lessons. See Larry Cuban, *Hugging the Middle; How Teachers Teach in an Age of Accountability* (New York: Teachers College Press, 2009), 24–25.

27. For Oakland Unified teachers, see my *Hugging the Middle*, 24–25. Another instance of school organizations adopting innovations and incorporating them into routine classroom, school, and district operations is the introduction of computers and other devices since the early 1980s and what has occurred since in using these devices. See Larry Cuban, *The Flight of the Butterfly or the Path of a Bullet: Using Technology to Transform Teaching and Learning* (Cambridge, MA: Harvard Education Press, 2018); Wikipedia, "Computers in Classrooms," at https:// en.wikipedia.org/wiki/Computers_in_the_classroom.

Index